Garfield's Thanksgiving

BY: JIM DAVIS

Ballantine Books • New York

GARFIELD'S THANKSGIVING is based on the television special written by Jim Davis, directed by Phil Roman, in association with United Media-Mendelson Productions © 1988 United Feature Syndicate, Inc.

 Published in the United States by Ballantine Books, a division of Random House, Inc., New York, and simultaneously in Canada by Random House of Canada Limited, Toronto.

Library of Congress Catalog Card Number: 88-91566
ISBN: 0-345-35650-0

Manufactured in the United States of America

First Edition: November 1988

10 9 8 7 6 5 4 3 2 1

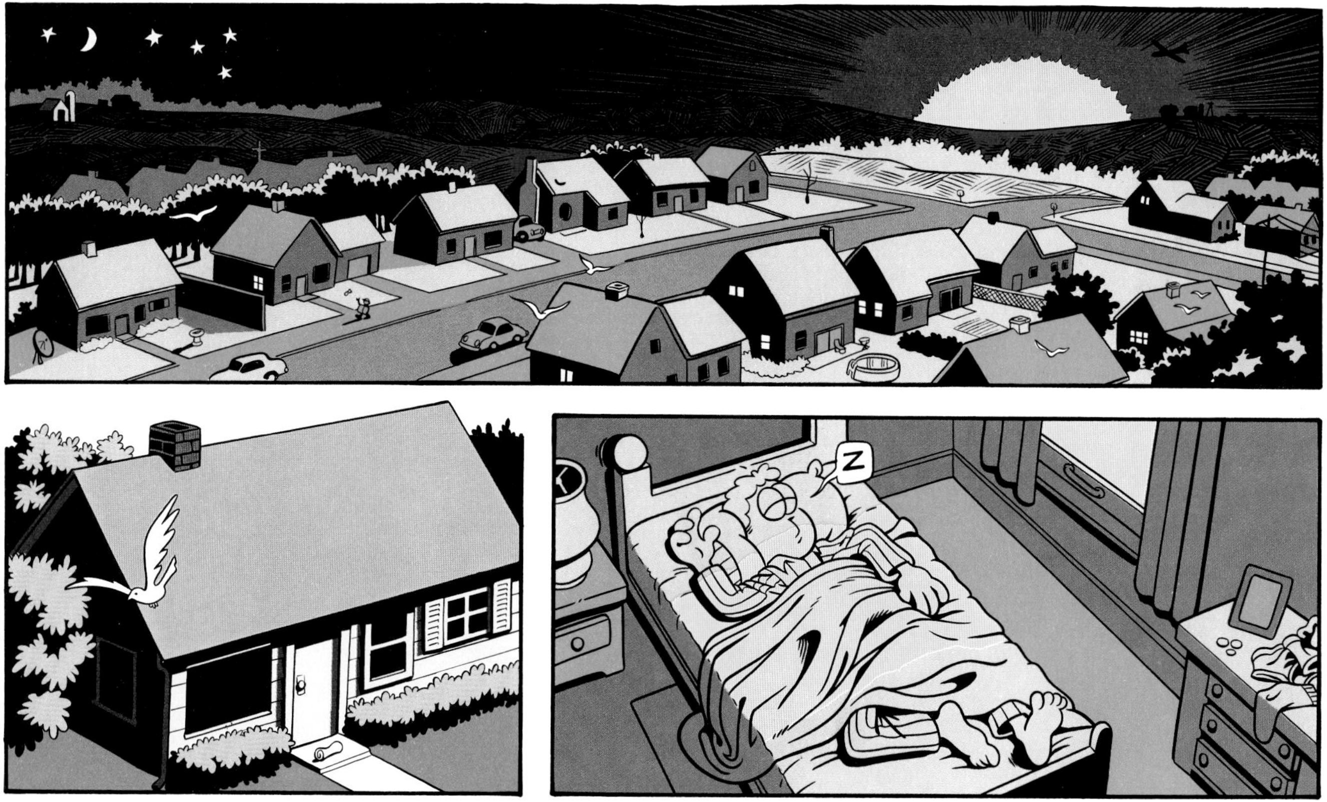
Z

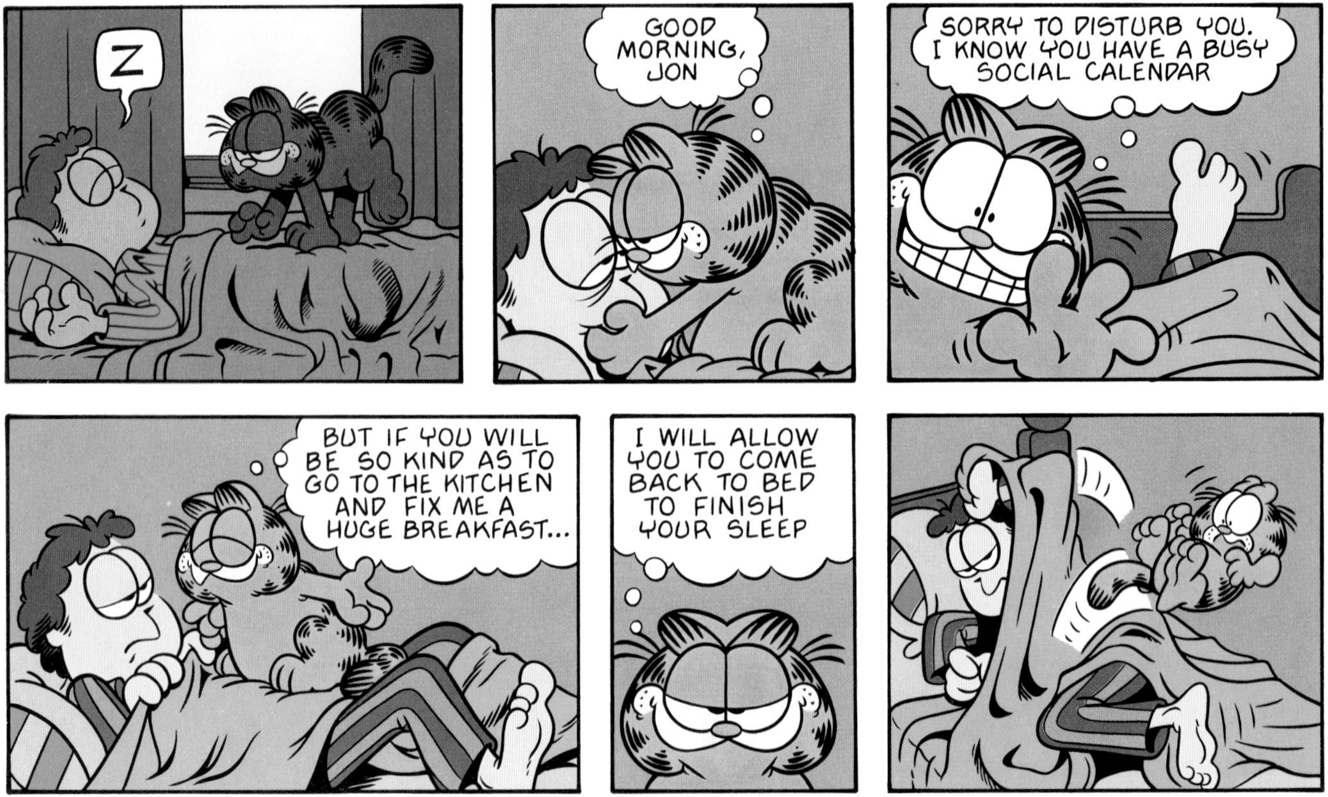
Z
GOOD MORNING, JON
SORRY TO DISTURB YOU. I KNOW YOU HAVE A BUSY SOCIAL CALENDAR
BUT IF YOU WILL BE SO KIND AS TO GO TO THE KITCHEN AND FIX ME A HUGE BREAKFAST...
I WILL ALLOW YOU TO COME BACK TO BED TO FINISH YOUR SLEEP

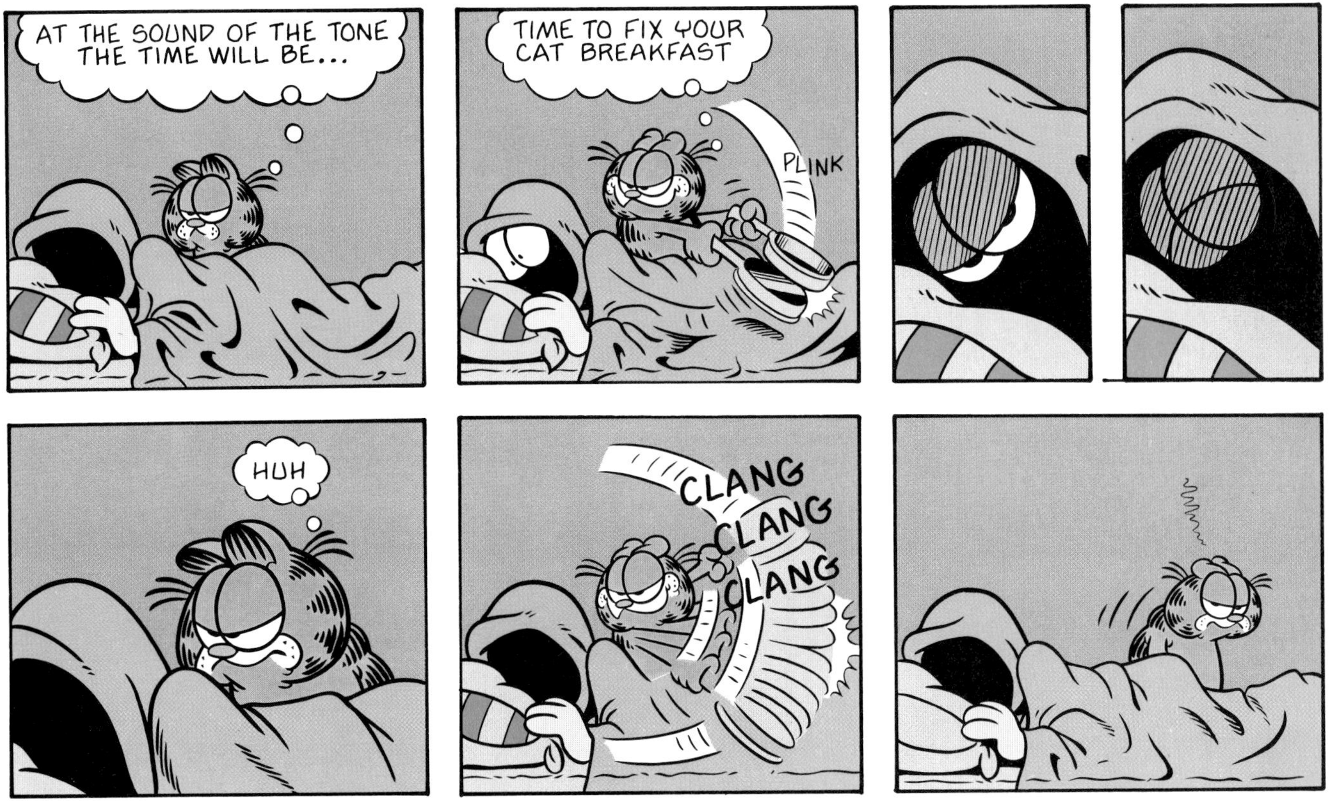
AT THE SOUND OF THE TONE THE TIME WILL BE...
TIME TO FIX YOUR CAT BREAKFAST
PLINK
HUH
CLANG
CLANG
CLANG

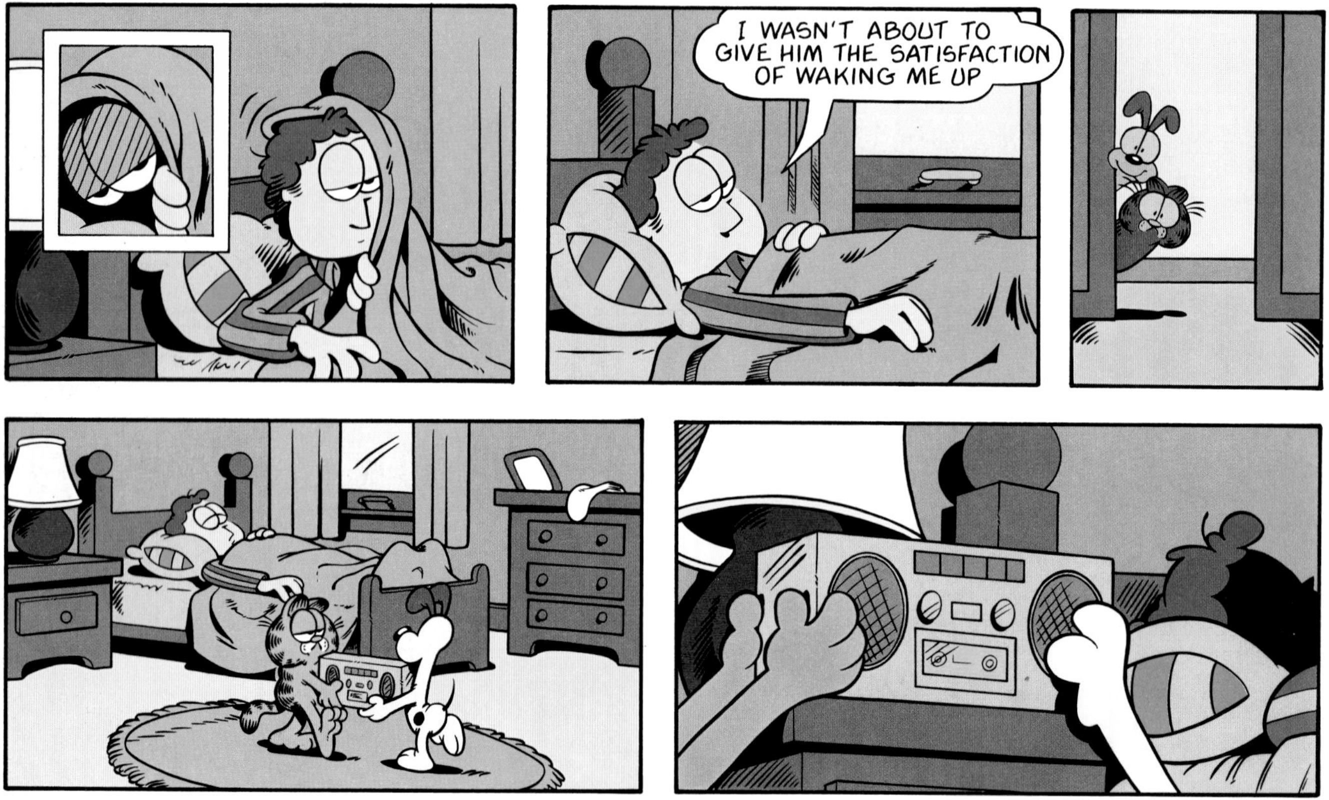
I WASN'T ABOUT TO GIVE HIM THE SATISFACTION OF WAKING ME UP

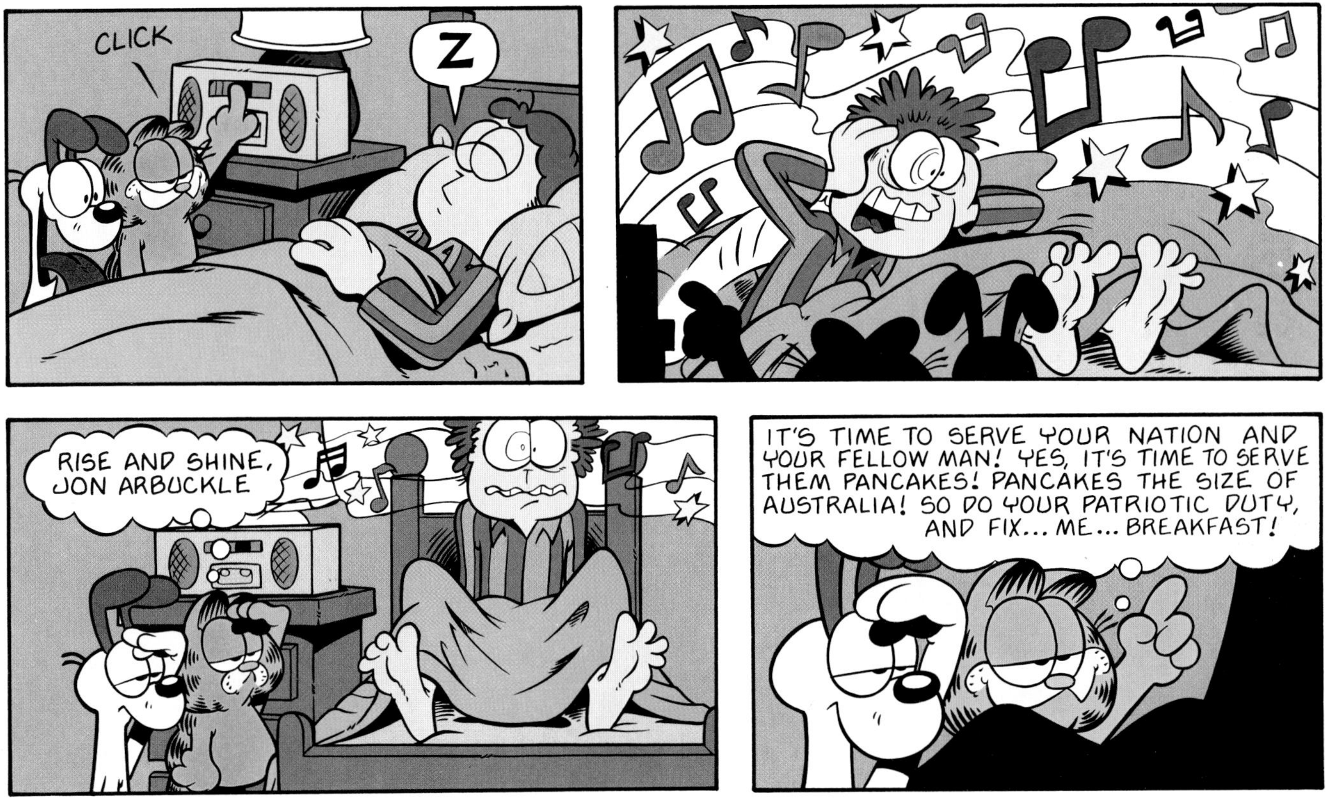
CLICK
Z
RISE AND SHINE, JON ARBUCKLE
IT'S TIME TO SERVE YOUR NATION AND YOUR FELLOW MAN! YES, IT'S TIME TO SERVE THEM PANCAKES! PANCAKES THE SIZE OF AUSTRALIA! SO DO YOUR PATRIOTIC DUTY, AND FIX... ME... BREAKFAST!

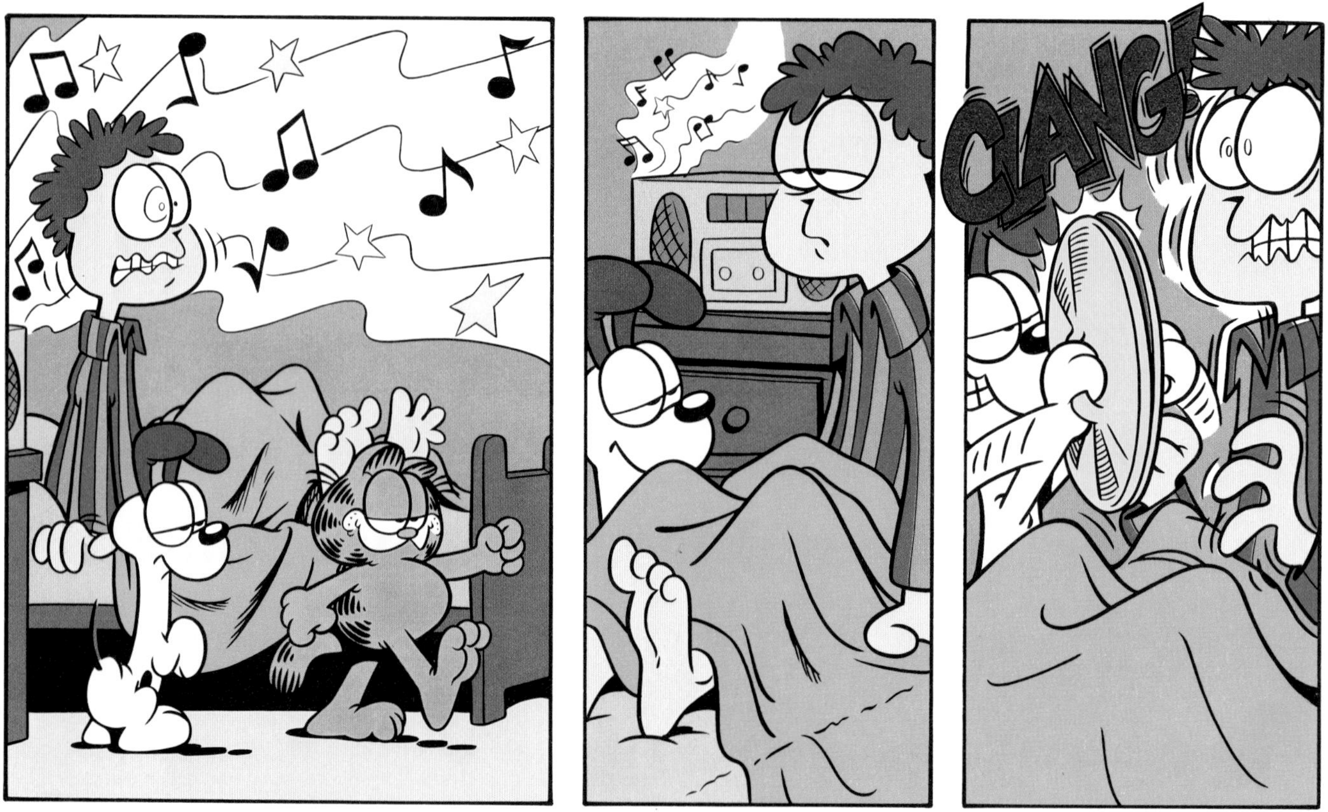
CLANG!

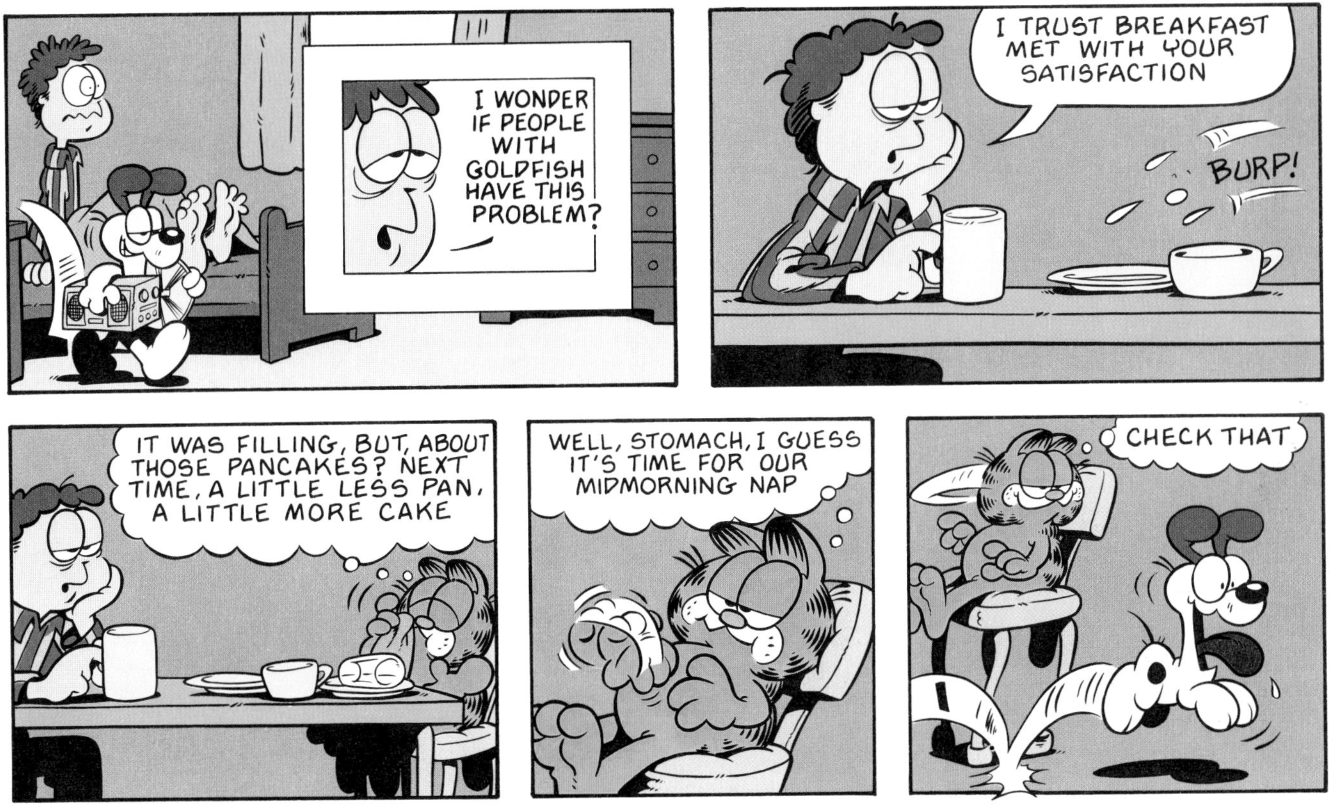
I WONDER IF PEOPLE WITH GOLDFISH HAVE THIS PROBLEM?
I TRUST BREAKFAST MET WITH YOUR SATISFACTION
BURP!
IT WAS FILLING, BUT, ABOUT THOSE PANCAKES? NEXT TIME, A LITTLE LESS PAN, A LITTLE MORE CAKE
WELL, STOMACH, I GUESS IT'S TIME FOR OUR MIDMORNING NAP
CHECK THAT

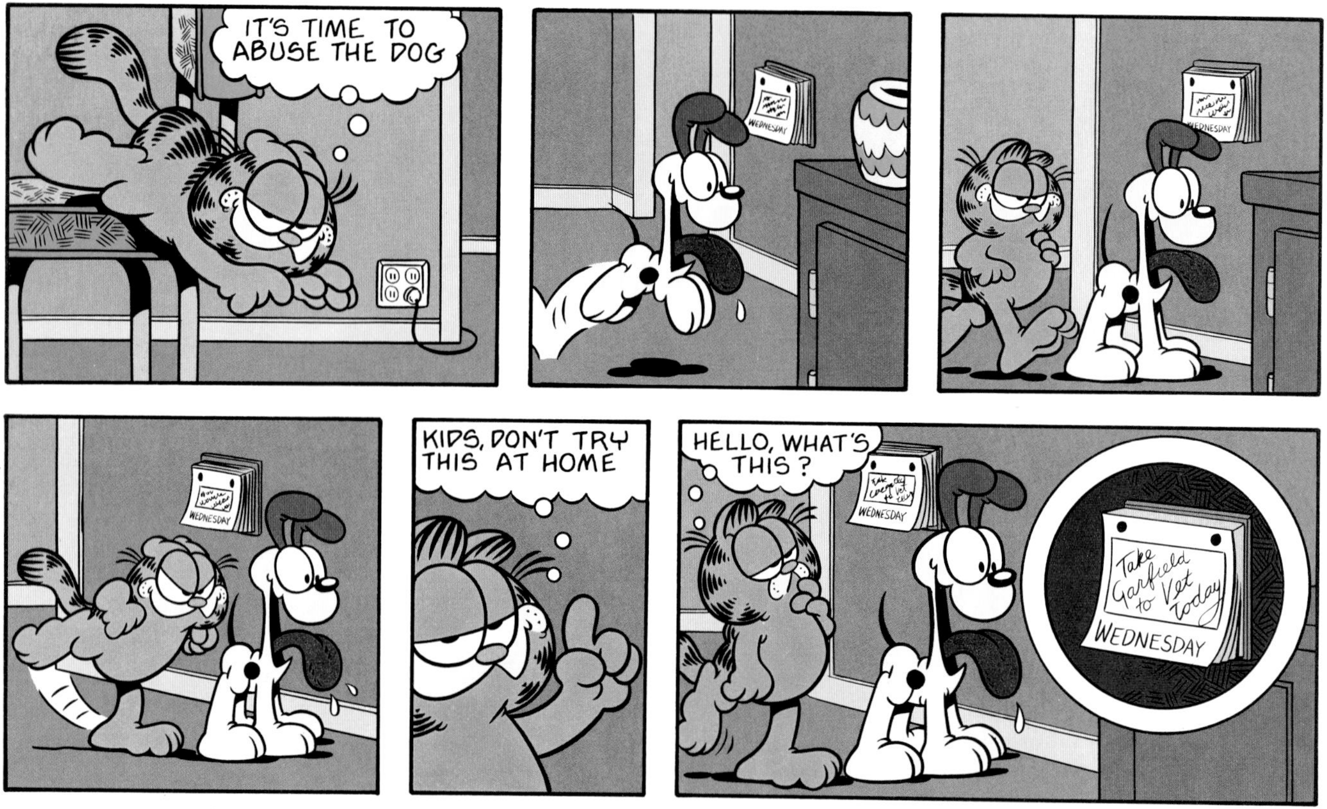
IT'S TIME TO ABUSE THE DOG
WEDNESDAY
KIDS, DON'T TRY THIS AT HOME
HELLO, WHAT'S THIS?
Take Garfield to Vet today
WEDNESDAY

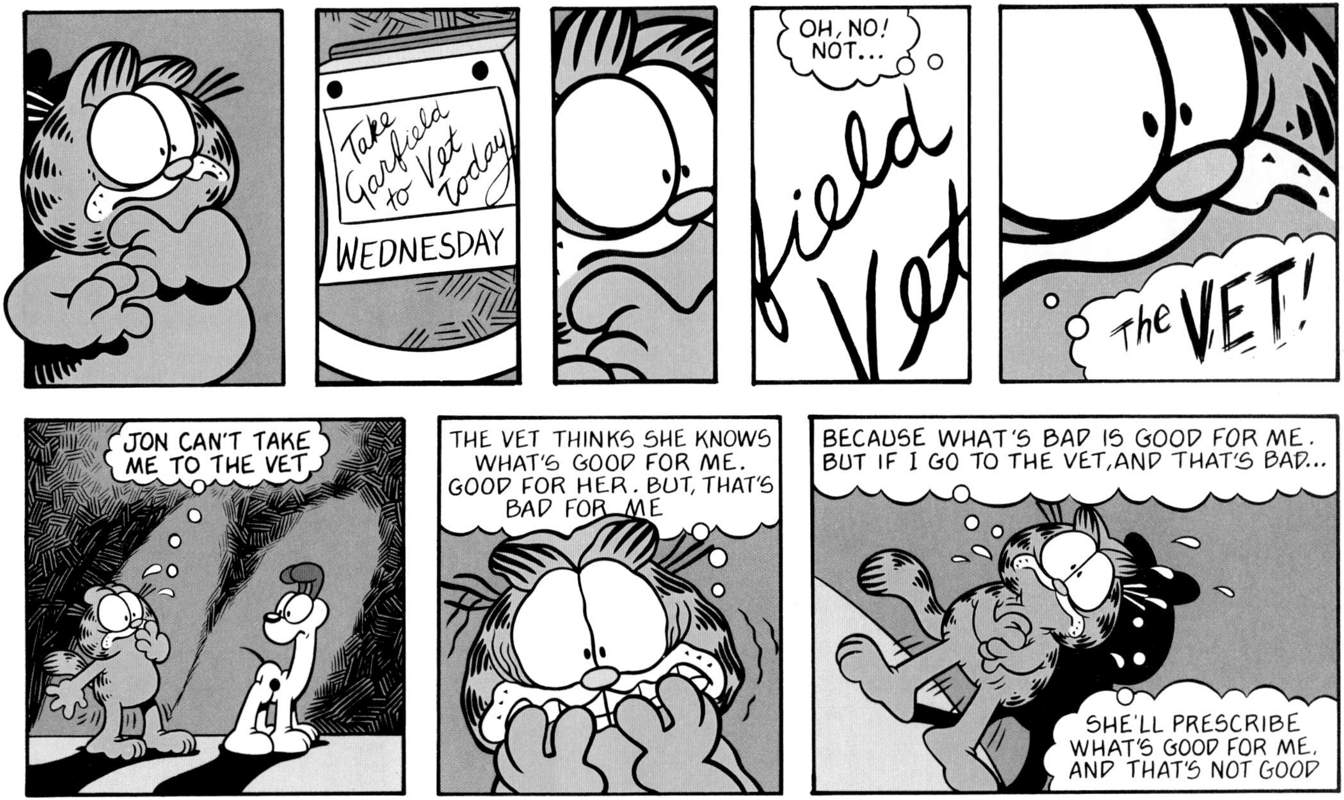
Take Garfield to Vet Today
WEDNESDAY
OH, NO! NOT...
field Vet
the VET!
JON CAN'T TAKE ME TO THE VET
THE VET THINKS SHE KNOWS WHAT'S GOOD FOR ME. GOOD FOR HER. BUT, THAT'S BAD FOR ME
BECAUSE WHAT'S BAD IS GOOD FOR ME. BUT IF I GO TO THE VET, AND THAT'S BAD...
SHE'LL PRESCRIBE WHAT'S GOOD FOR ME, AND THAT'S NOT GOOD

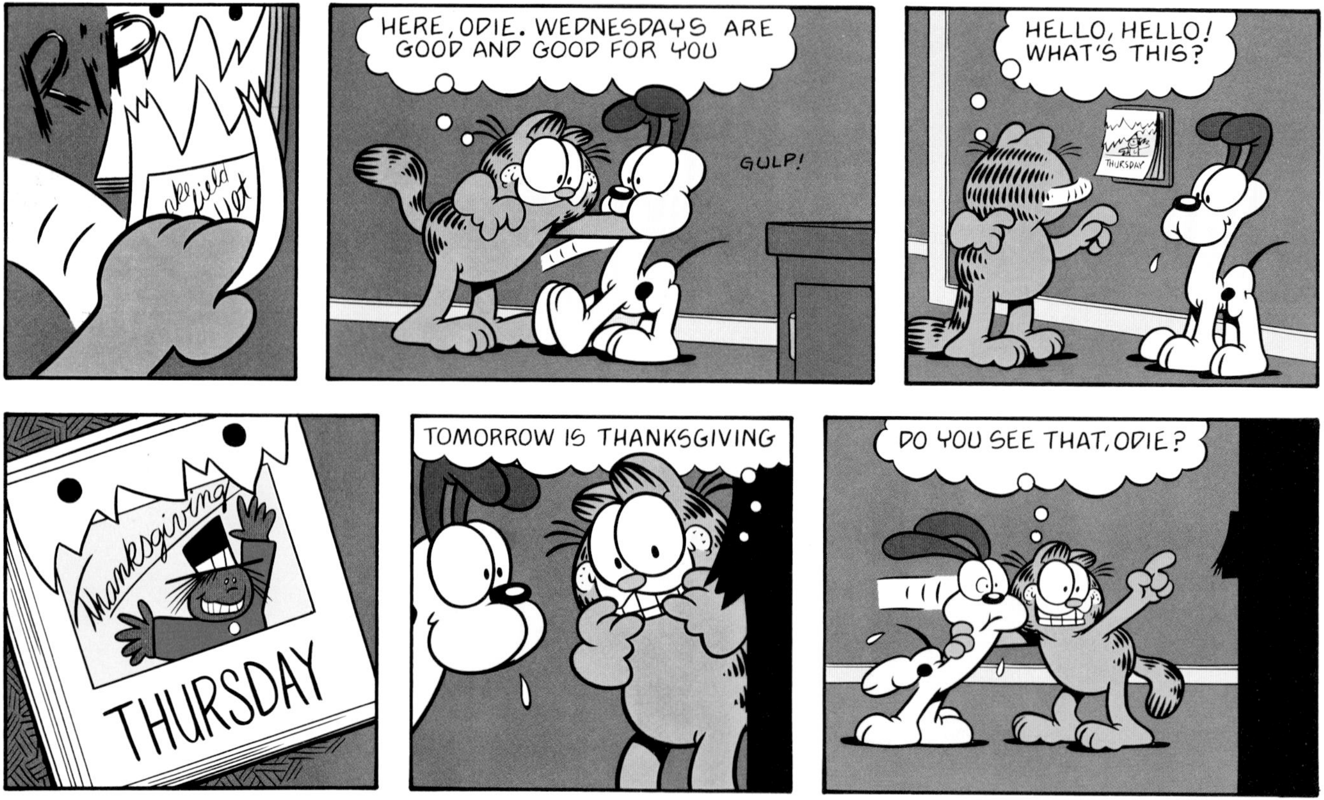
RIP
HERE, ODIE. WEDNESDAYS ARE GOOD AND GOOD FOR YOU
GULP!
HELLO, HELLO! WHAT'S THIS?
THURSDAY
Thanksgiving
THURSDAY
TOMORROW IS THANKSGIVING
DO YOU SEE THAT, ODIE?

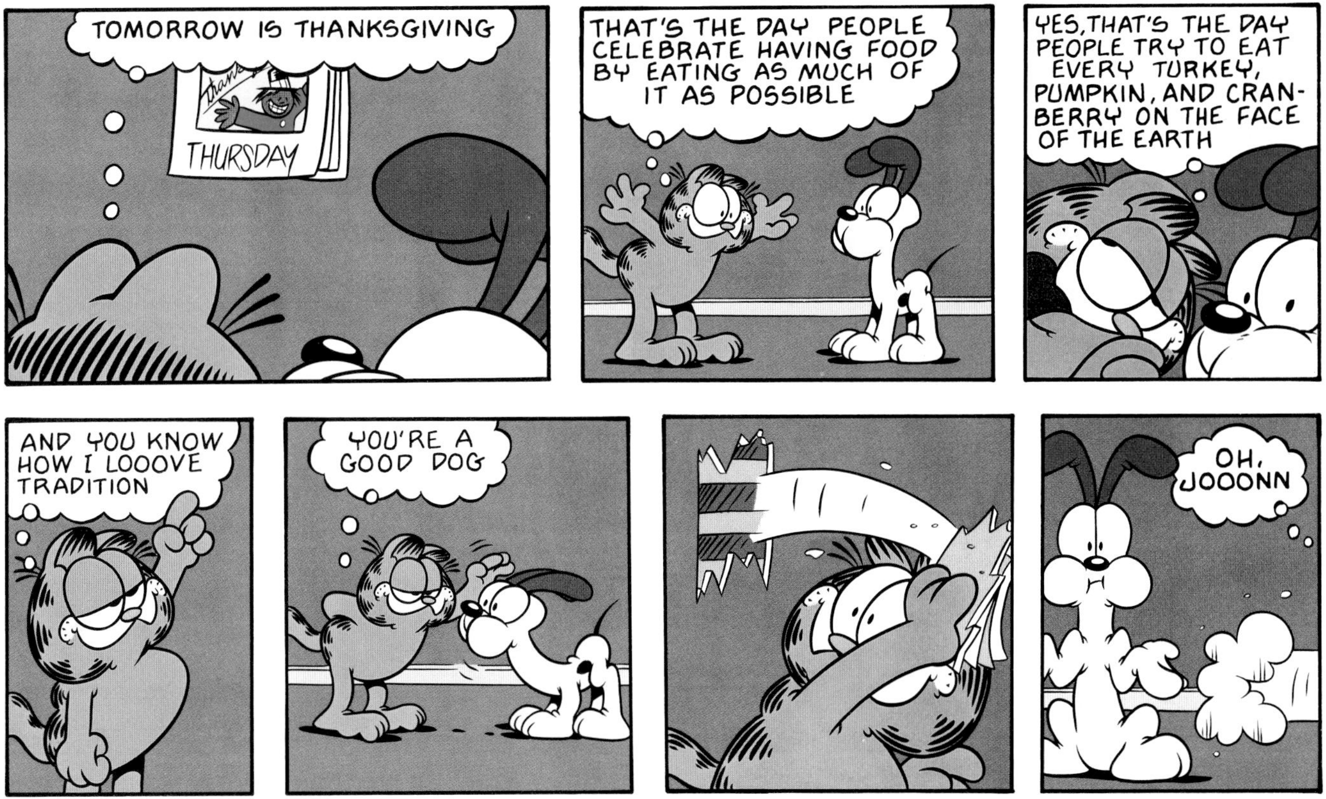
TOMORROW IS THANKSGIVING
THURSDAY
THAT'S THE DAY PEOPLE CELEBRATE HAVING FOOD BY EATING AS MUCH OF IT AS POSSIBLE
YES, THAT'S THE DAY PEOPLE TRY TO EAT EVERY TURKEY, PUMPKIN, AND CRAN-BERRY ON THE FACE OF THE EARTH
AND YOU KNOW HOW I LOOOVE TRADITION
YOU'RE A GOOD DOG
OH, JOOONN

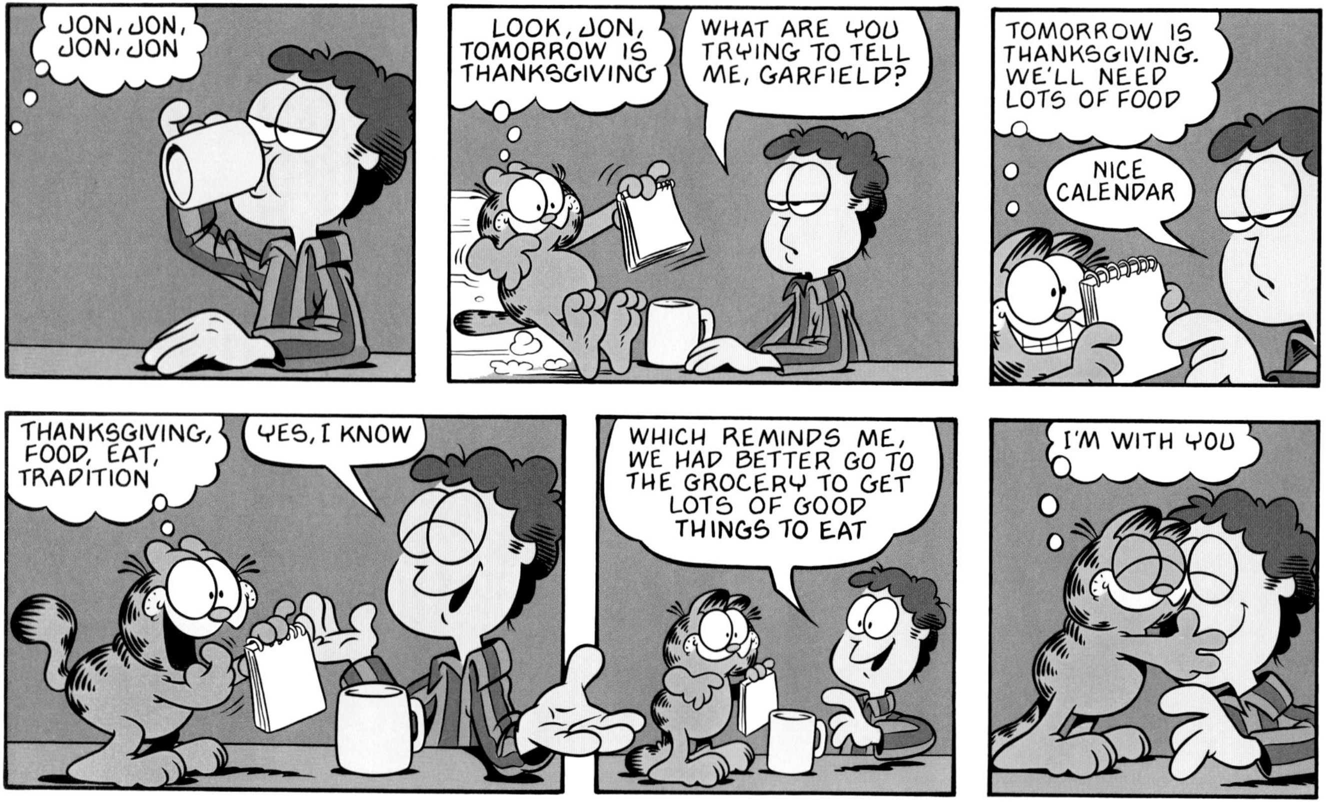
JON, JON, JON, JON
LOOK, JON, TOMORROW IS THANKSGIVING
WHAT ARE YOU TRYING TO TELL ME, GARFIELD?
TOMORROW IS THANKSGIVING. WE'LL NEED LOTS OF FOOD
NICE CALENDAR
THANKSGIVING, FOOD, EAT, TRADITION
YES, I KNOW
WHICH REMINDS ME, WE HAD BETTER GO TO THE GROCERY TO GET LOTS OF GOOD THINGS TO EAT
I'M WITH YOU

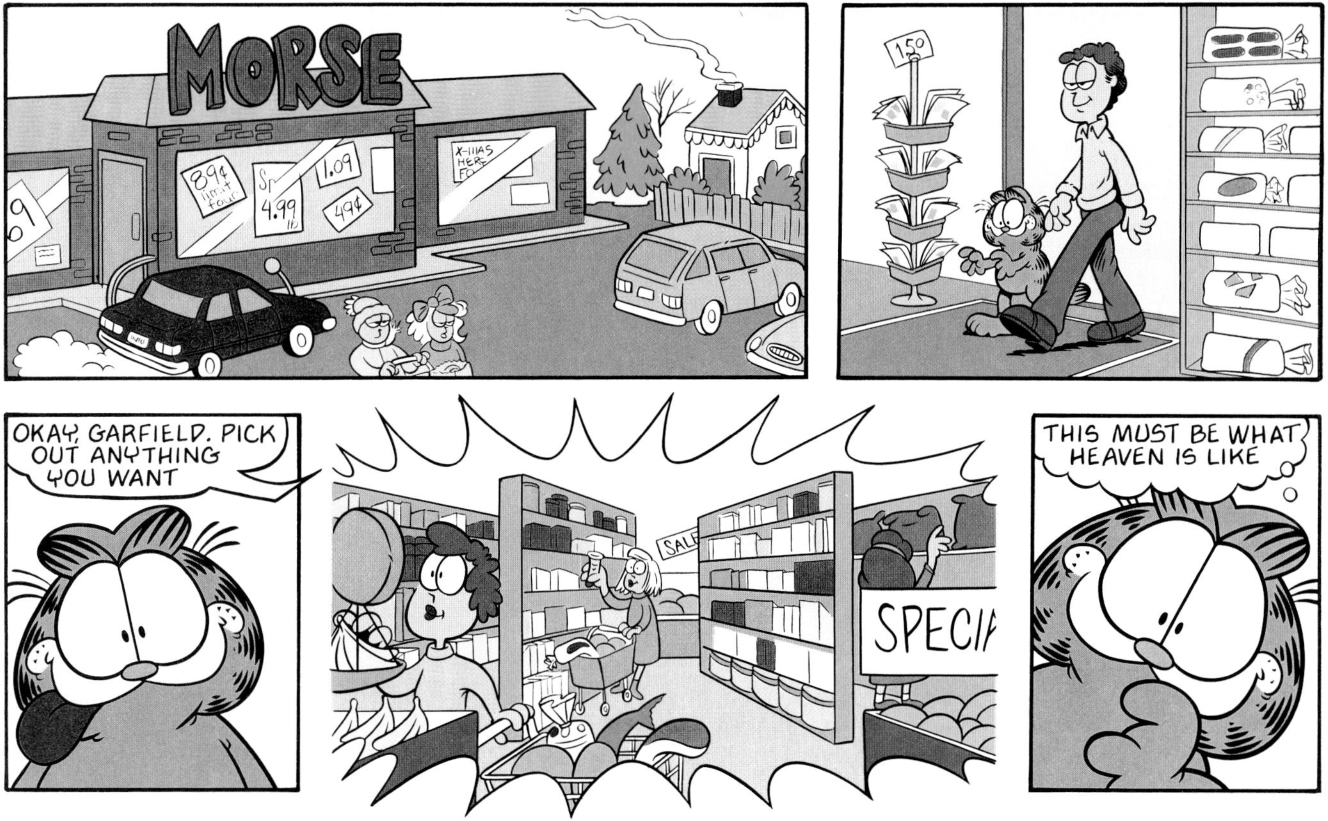
MORSE
89¢ limit four
4.99 lb
1.09
49¢
150
OKAY, GARFIELD. PICK OUT ANYTHING YOU WANT
SPECI
THIS MUST BE WHAT HEAVEN IS LIKE

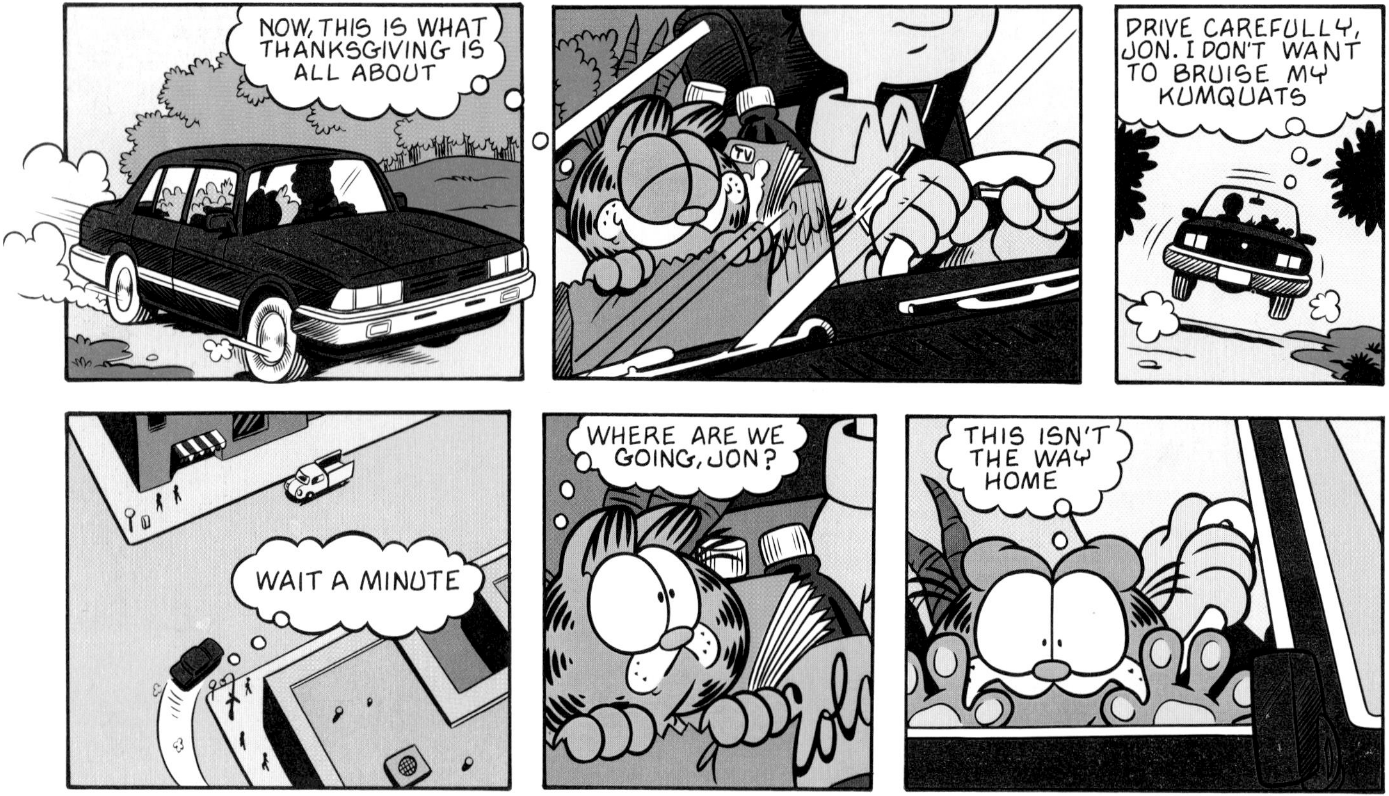
NOW, THIS IS WHAT THANKSGIVING IS ALL ABOUT
DRIVE CAREFULLY, JON. I DON'T WANT TO BRUISE MY KUMQUATS
WAIT A MINUTE
WHERE ARE WE GOING, JON?
THIS ISN'T THE WAY HOME

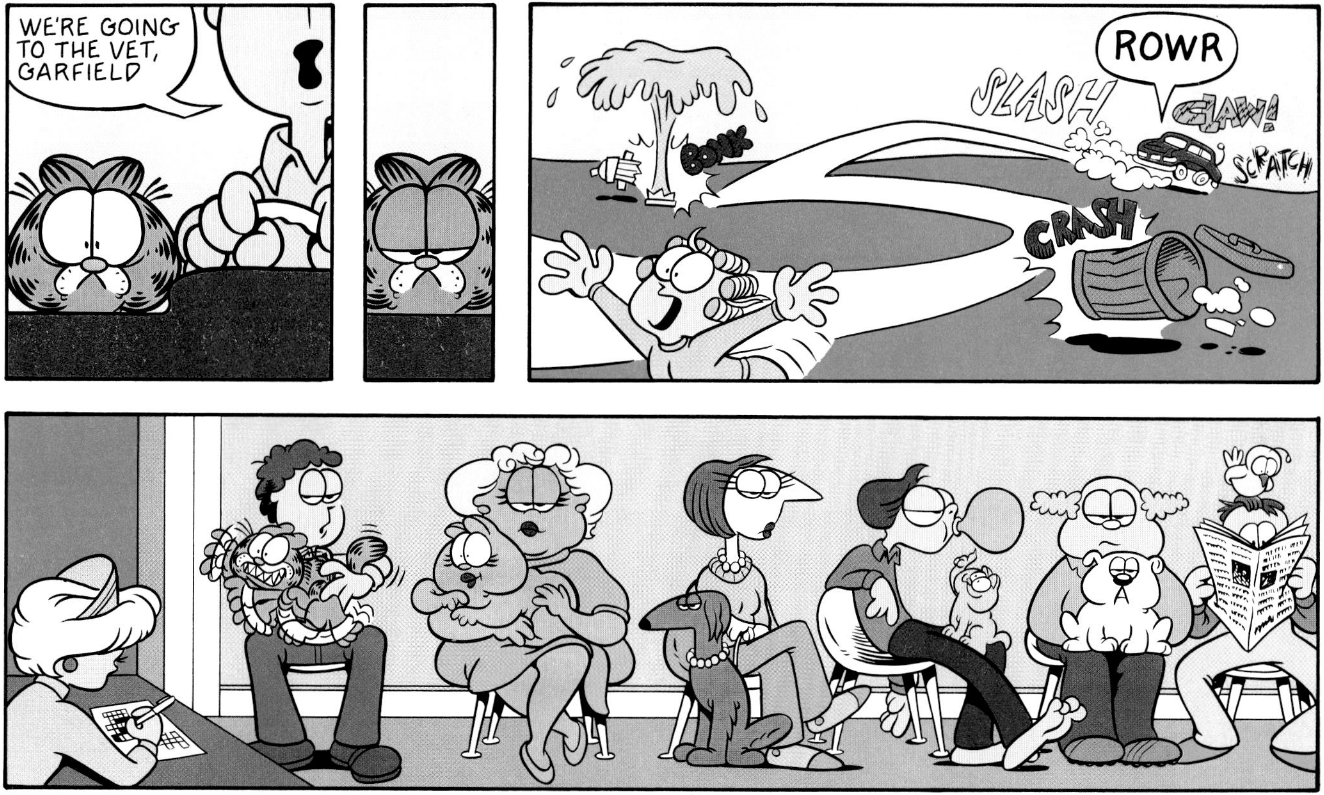
WE'RE GOING TO THE VET, GARFIELD
BONK
SLASH
ROWR
CLAW!
SCRATCH!
CRASH

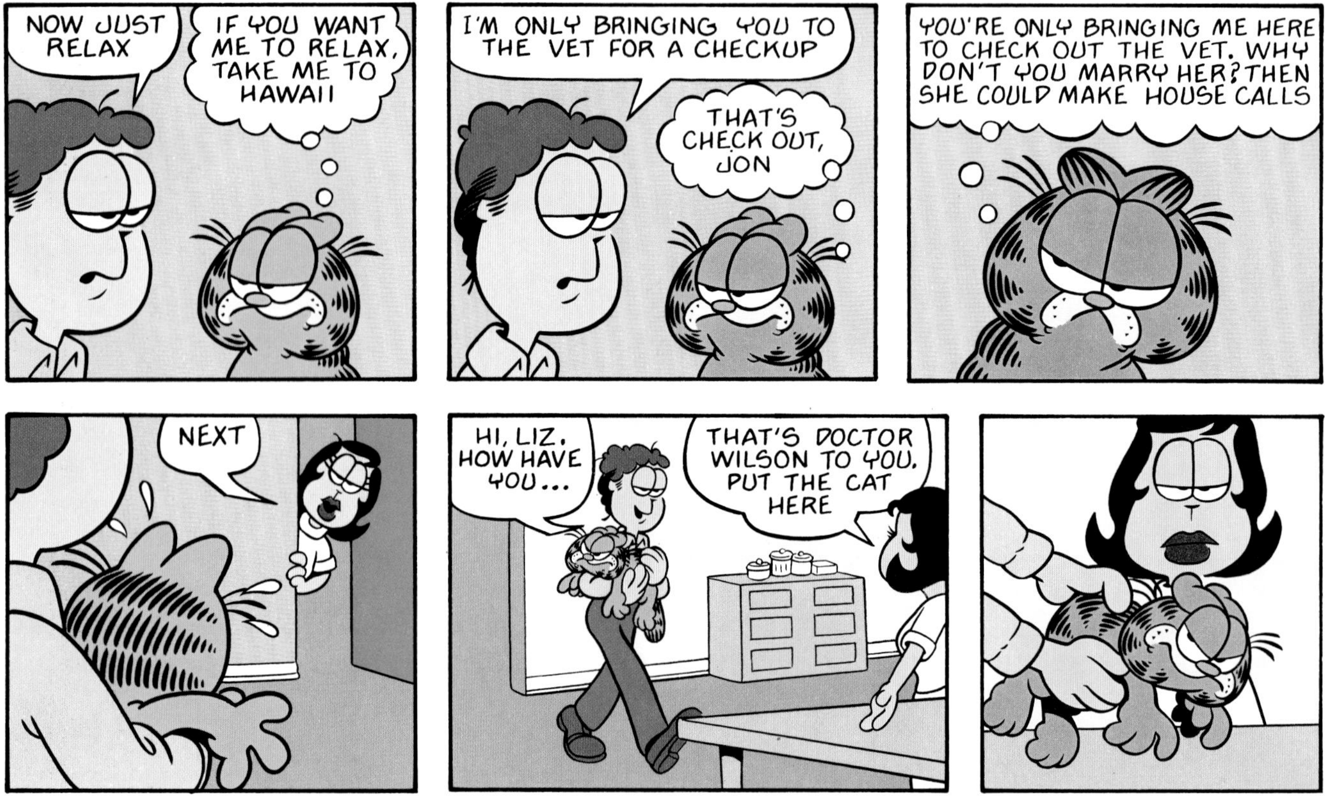
NOW JUST RELAX
IF YOU WANT ME TO RELAX, TAKE ME TO HAWAII
I'M ONLY BRINGING YOU TO THE VET FOR A CHECKUP
THAT'S CHECK OUT, JON
YOU'RE ONLY BRINGING ME HERE TO CHECK OUT THE VET. WHY DON'T YOU MARRY HER? THEN SHE COULD MAKE HOUSE CALLS
NEXT
HI, LIZ. HOW HAVE YOU...
THAT'S DOCTOR WILSON TO YOU. PUT THE CAT HERE

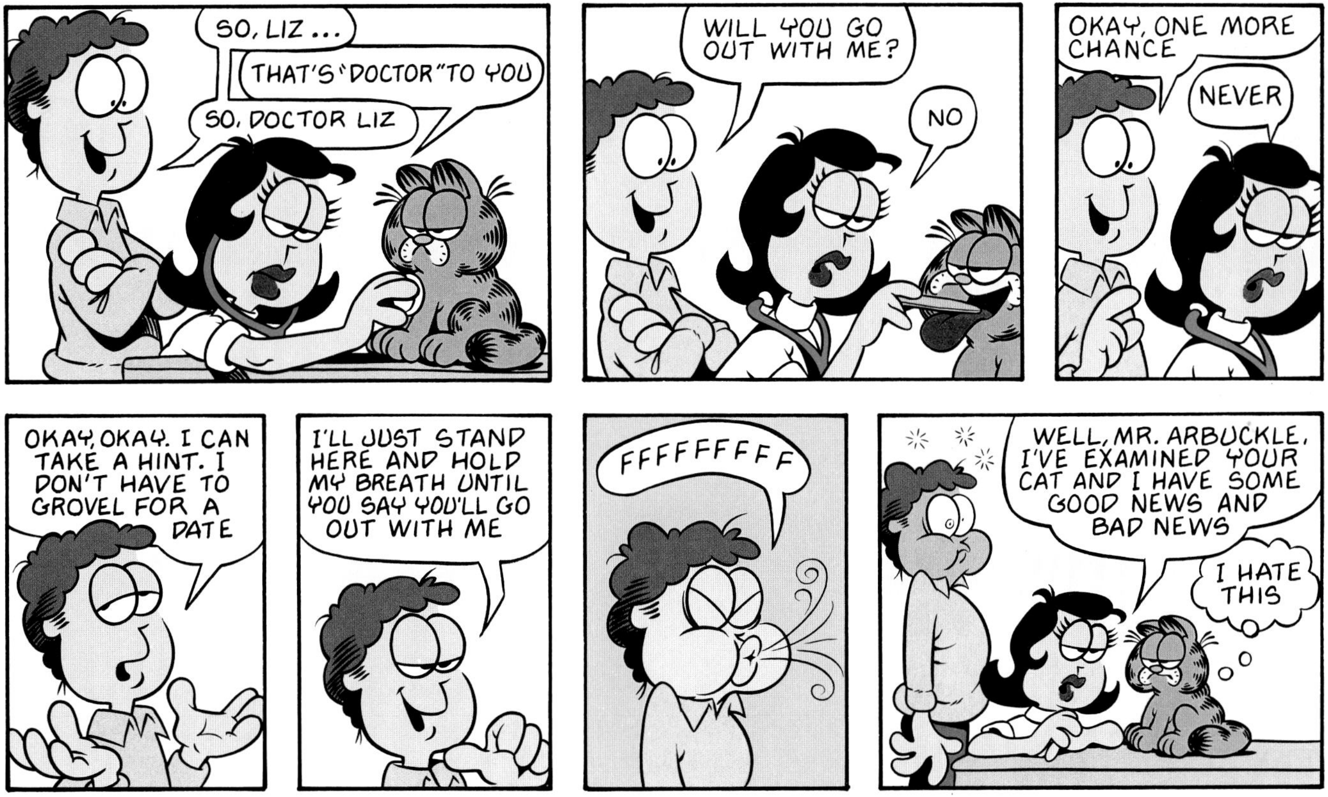
SO, LIZ ...
THAT'S "DOCTOR" TO YOU
SO, DOCTOR LIZ
WILL YOU GO OUT WITH ME?
NO
OKAY, ONE MORE CHANCE
NEVER
OKAY, OKAY. I CAN TAKE A HINT. I DON'T HAVE TO GROVEL FOR A DATE
I'LL JUST STAND HERE AND HOLD MY BREATH UNTIL YOU SAY YOU'LL GO OUT WITH ME
FFFFFFFFF
WELL, MR. ARBUCKLE, I'VE EXAMINED YOUR CAT AND I HAVE SOME GOOD NEWS AND BAD NEWS
I HATE THIS

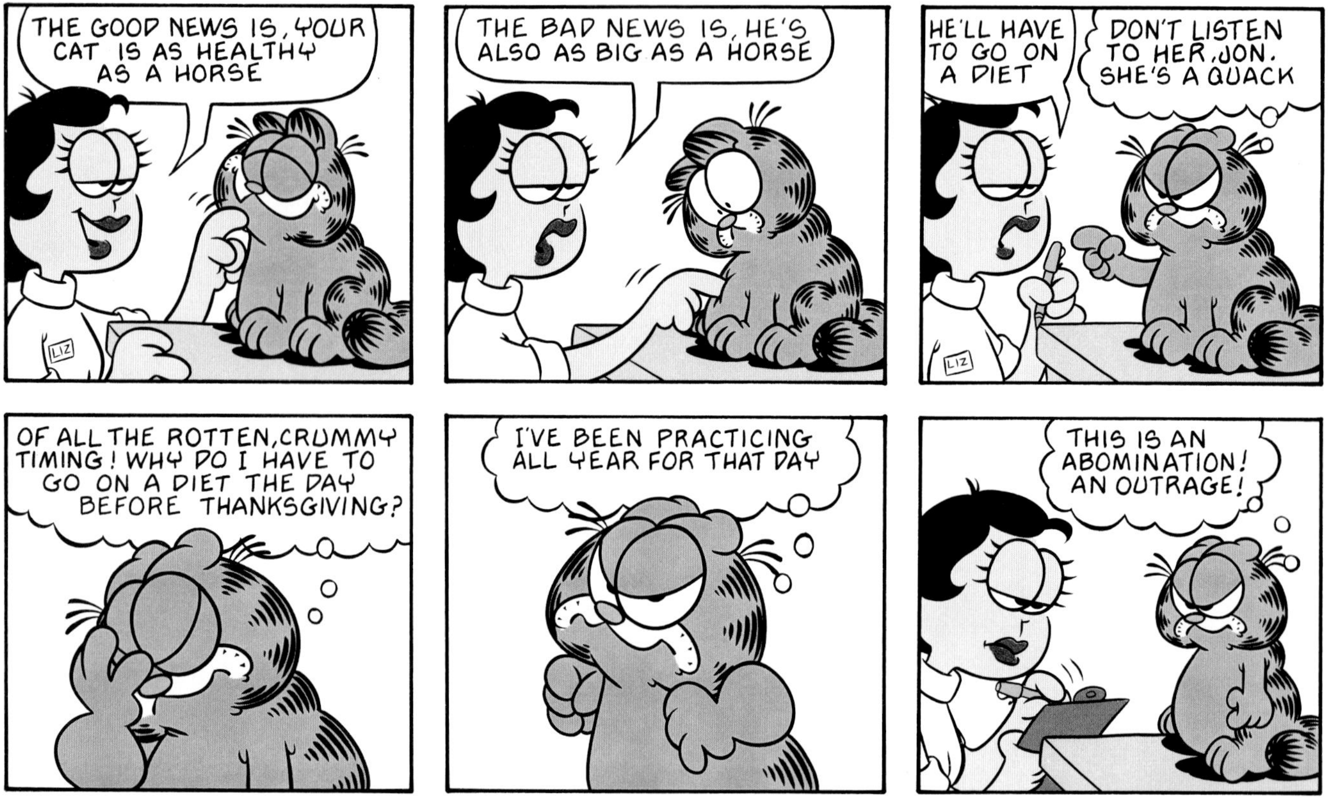
THE GOOD NEWS IS, YOUR CAT IS AS HEALTHY AS A HORSE
LIZ
THE BAD NEWS IS, HE'S ALSO AS BIG AS A HORSE
HE'LL HAVE TO GO ON A DIET
DON'T LISTEN TO HER, JON. SHE'S A QUACK
LIZ
OF ALL THE ROTTEN, CRUMMY TIMING! WHY DO I HAVE TO GO ON A DIET THE DAY BEFORE THANKSGIVING?
I'VE BEEN PRACTICING ALL YEAR FOR THAT DAY
THIS IS AN ABOMINATION! AN OUTRAGE!

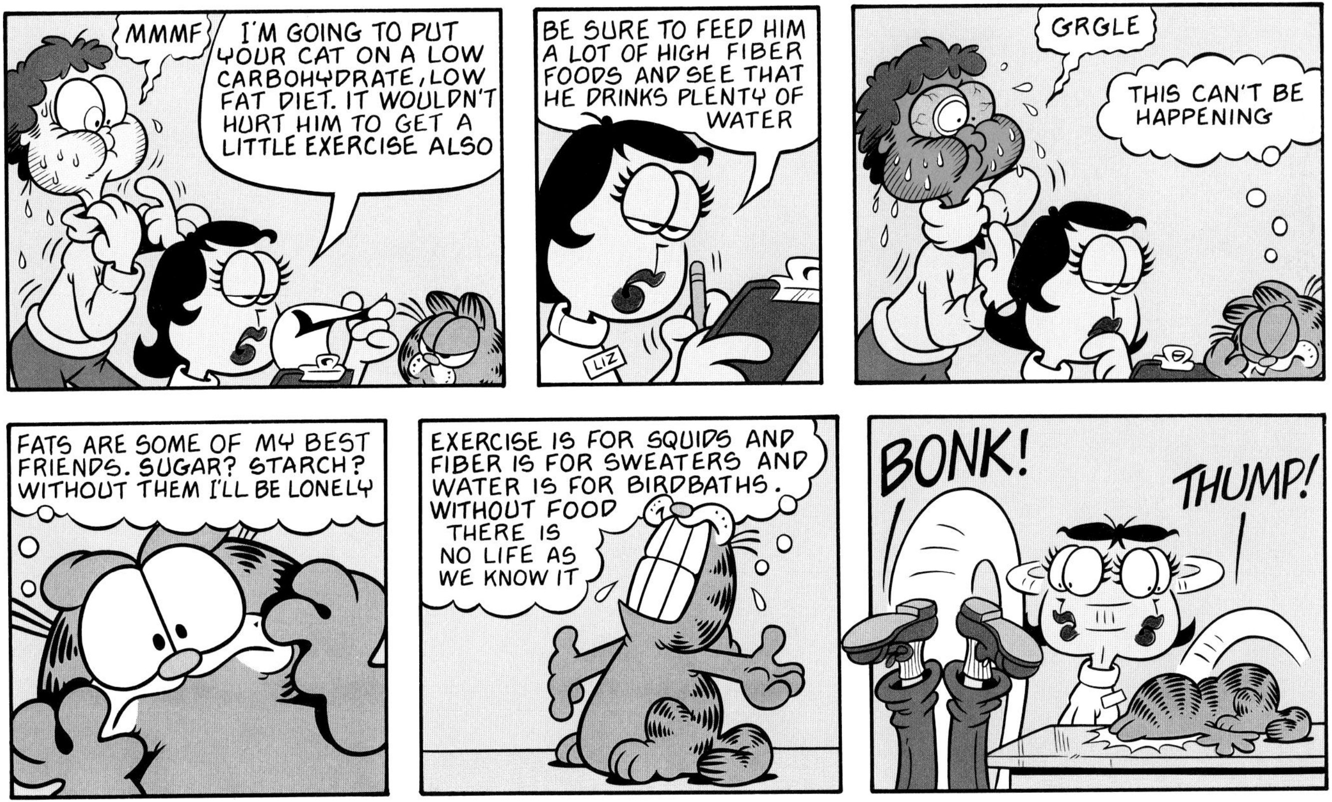
MMMF
I'M GOING TO PUT YOUR CAT ON A LOW CARBOHYDRATE, LOW FAT DIET. IT WOULDN'T HURT HIM TO GET A LITTLE EXERCISE ALSO
BE SURE TO FEED HIM A LOT OF HIGH FIBER FOODS AND SEE THAT HE DRINKS PLENTY OF WATER
LIZ
GRGLE
THIS CAN'T BE HAPPENING
FATS ARE SOME OF MY BEST FRIENDS. SUGAR? STARCH? WITHOUT THEM I'LL BE LONELY
EXERCISE IS FOR SQUIDS AND FIBER IS FOR SWEATERS AND WATER IS FOR BIRDBATHS. WITHOUT FOOD THERE IS NO LIFE AS WE KNOW IT
BONK!
THUMP!

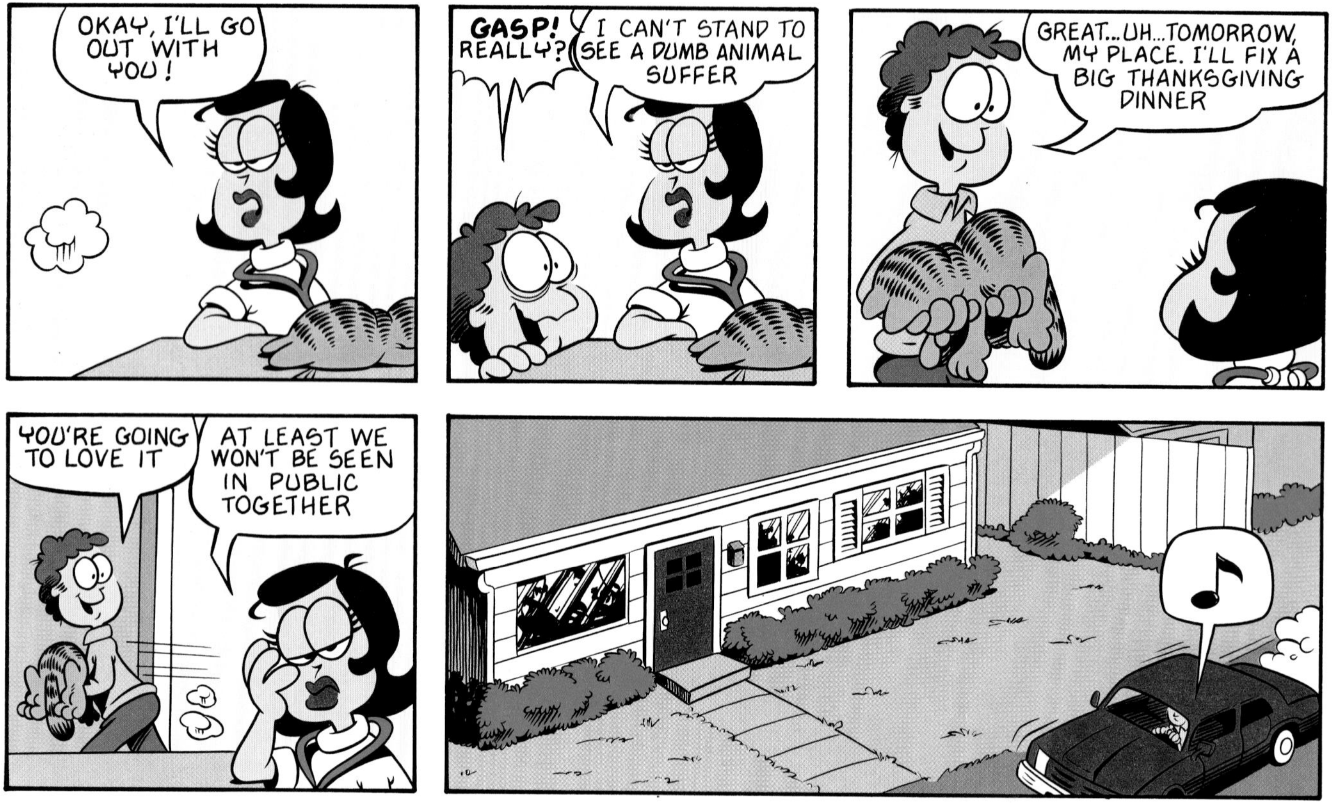
OKAY, I'LL GO OUT WITH YOU!
GASP! REALLY?
I CAN'T STAND TO SEE A DUMB ANIMAL SUFFER
GREAT...UH...TOMORROW, MY PLACE. I'LL FIX A BIG THANKSGIVING DINNER
YOU'RE GOING TO LOVE IT
AT LEAST WE WON'T BE SEEN IN PUBLIC TOGETHER

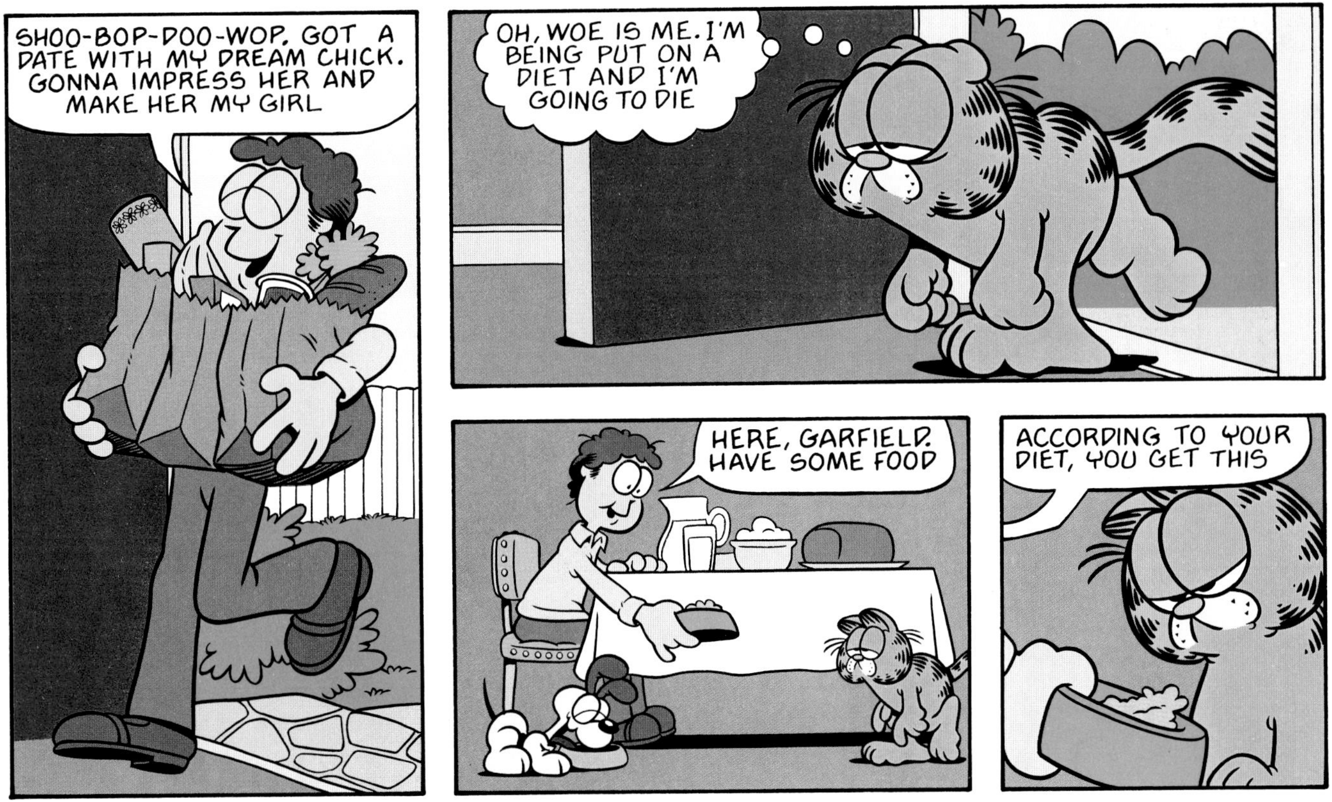
SHOO-BOP-DOO-WOP. GOT A DATE WITH MY DREAM CHICK. GONNA IMPRESS HER AND MAKE HER MY GIRL
OH, WOE IS ME. I'M BEING PUT ON A DIET AND I'M GOING TO DIE
HERE, GARFIELD. HAVE SOME FOOD
ACCORDING TO YOUR DIET, YOU GET THIS

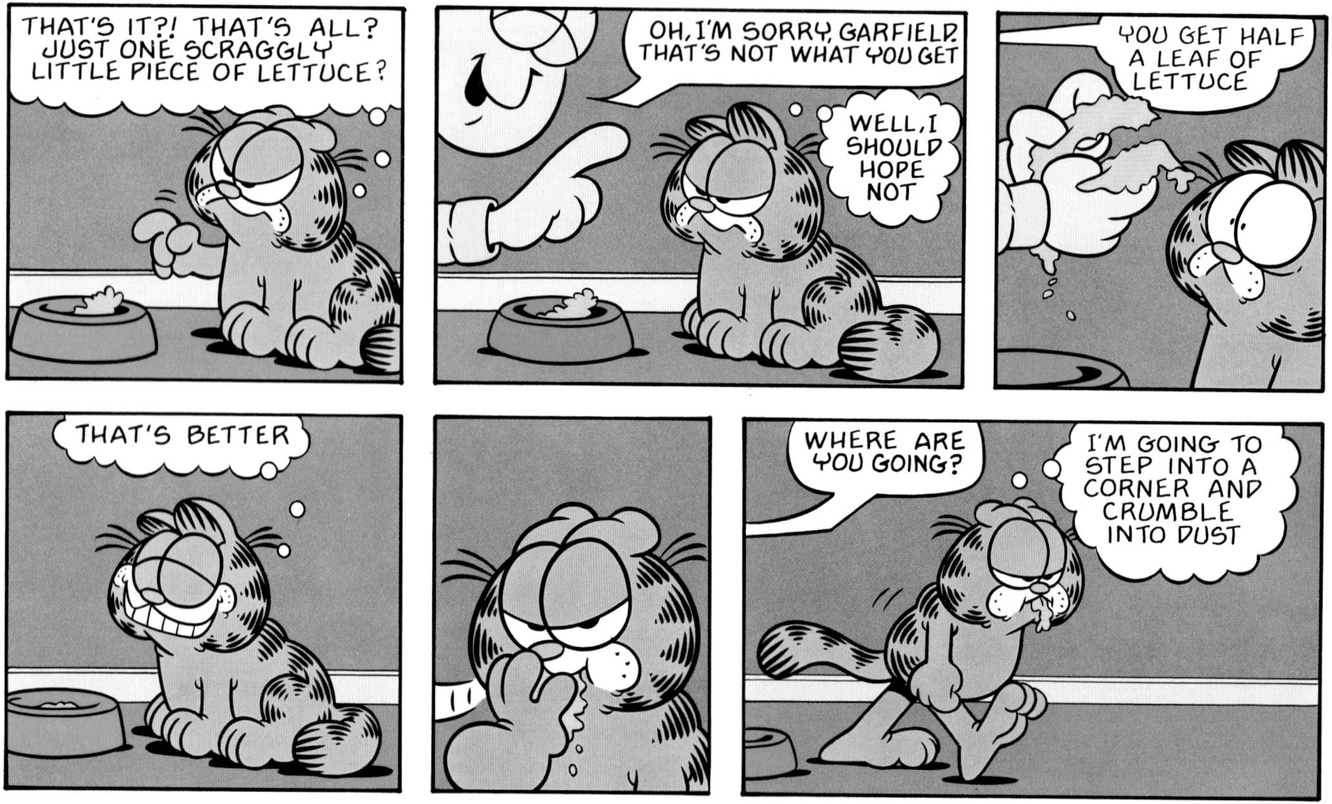
THAT'S IT?! THAT'S ALL? JUST ONE SCRAGGLY LITTLE PIECE OF LETTUCE?
OH, I'M SORRY, GARFIELD. THAT'S NOT WHAT YOU GET
WELL, I SHOULD HOPE NOT
YOU GET HALF A LEAF OF LETTUCE
THAT'S BETTER
WHERE ARE YOU GOING?
I'M GOING TO STEP INTO A CORNER AND CRUMBLE INTO DUST

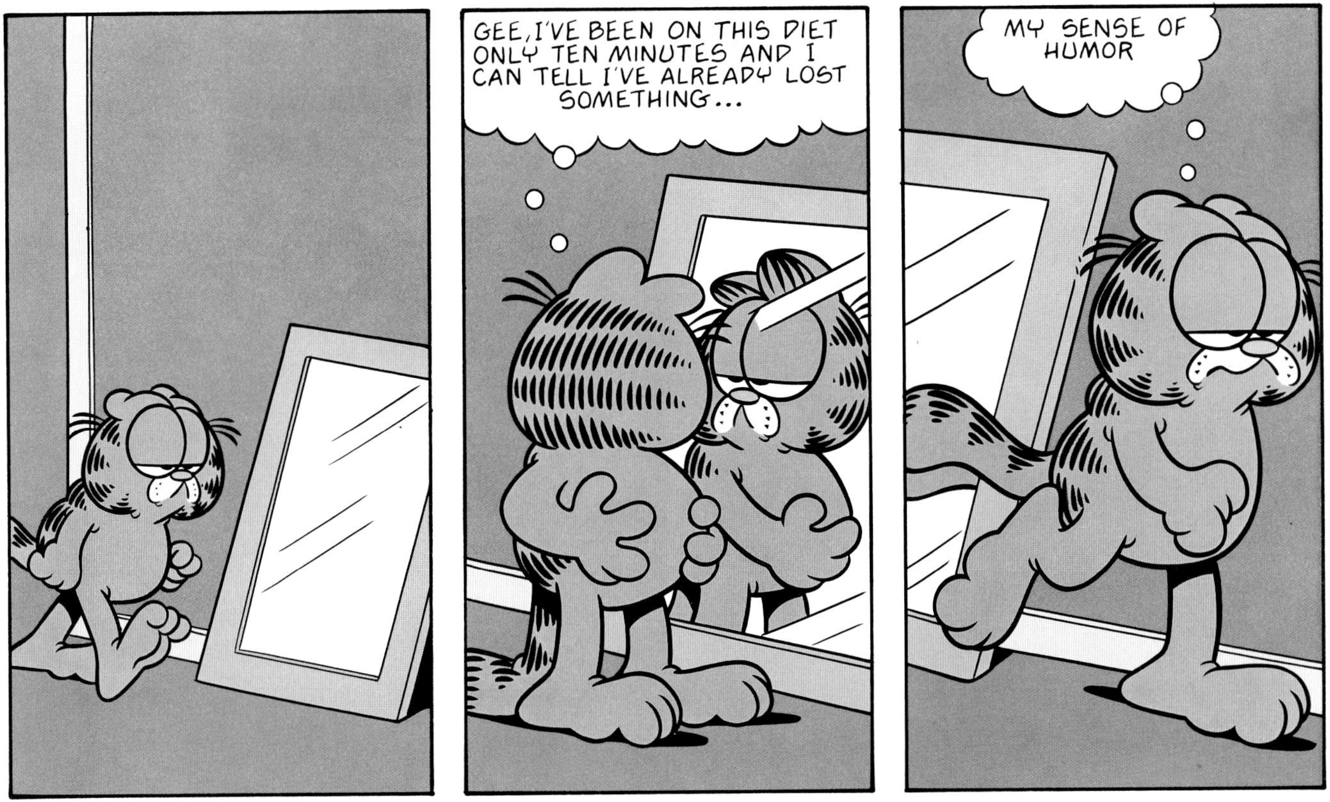
GEE, I'VE BEEN ON THIS DIET ONLY TEN MINUTES AND I CAN TELL I'VE ALREADY LOST SOMETHING...
MY SENSE OF HUMOR

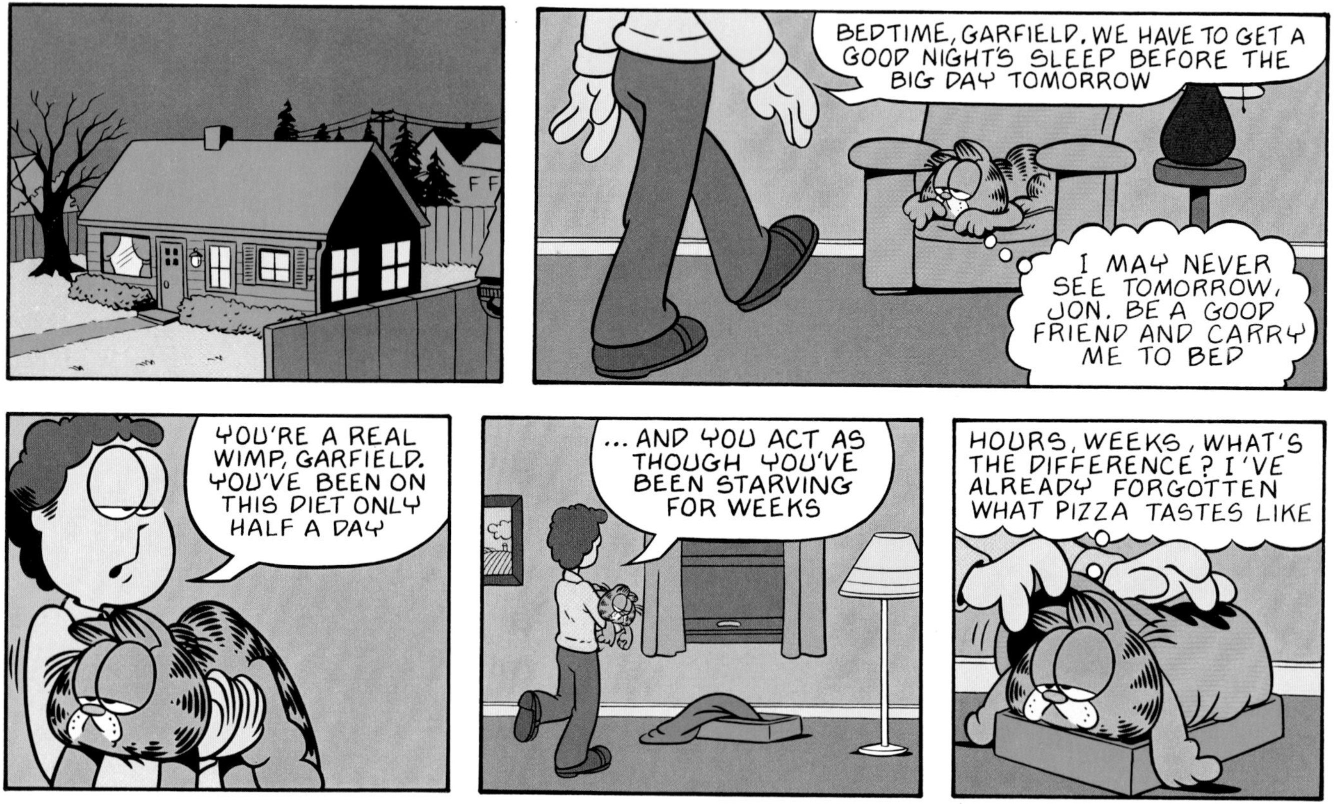
BEDTIME, GARFIELD. WE HAVE TO GET A GOOD NIGHT'S SLEEP BEFORE THE BIG DAY TOMORROW
I MAY NEVER SEE TOMORROW, JON. BE A GOOD FRIEND AND CARRY ME TO BED
YOU'RE A REAL WIMP, GARFIELD. YOU'VE BEEN ON THIS DIET ONLY HALF A DAY
...AND YOU ACT AS THOUGH YOU'VE BEEN STARVING FOR WEEKS
HOURS, WEEKS, WHAT'S THE DIFFERENCE? I'VE ALREADY FORGOTTEN WHAT PIZZA TASTES LIKE

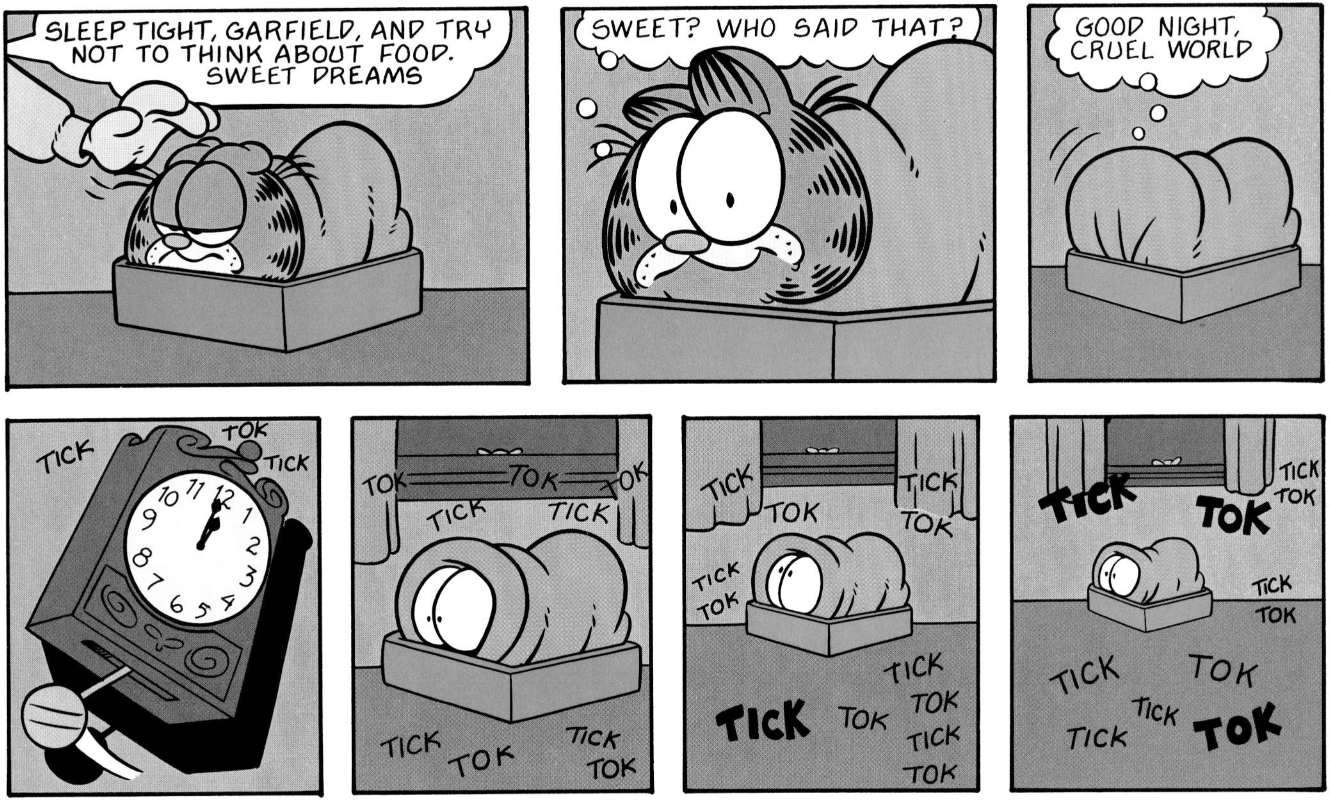
SLEEP TIGHT, GARFIELD, AND TRY NOT TO THINK ABOUT FOOD. SWEET DREAMS
SWEET? WHO SAID THAT?
GOOD NIGHT, CRUEL WORLD
TICK
TOK
TICK
TOK TOK TOK
TICK TICK
TICK TOK
TICK TOK
TICK TOK
TICK TICK
TOK TOK
TICK TOK
TICK TOK
TICK TOK TICK TOK
TICK TOK
TICK TOK
TICK TOK
TICK TOK
TICK TICK TOK TICK TOK

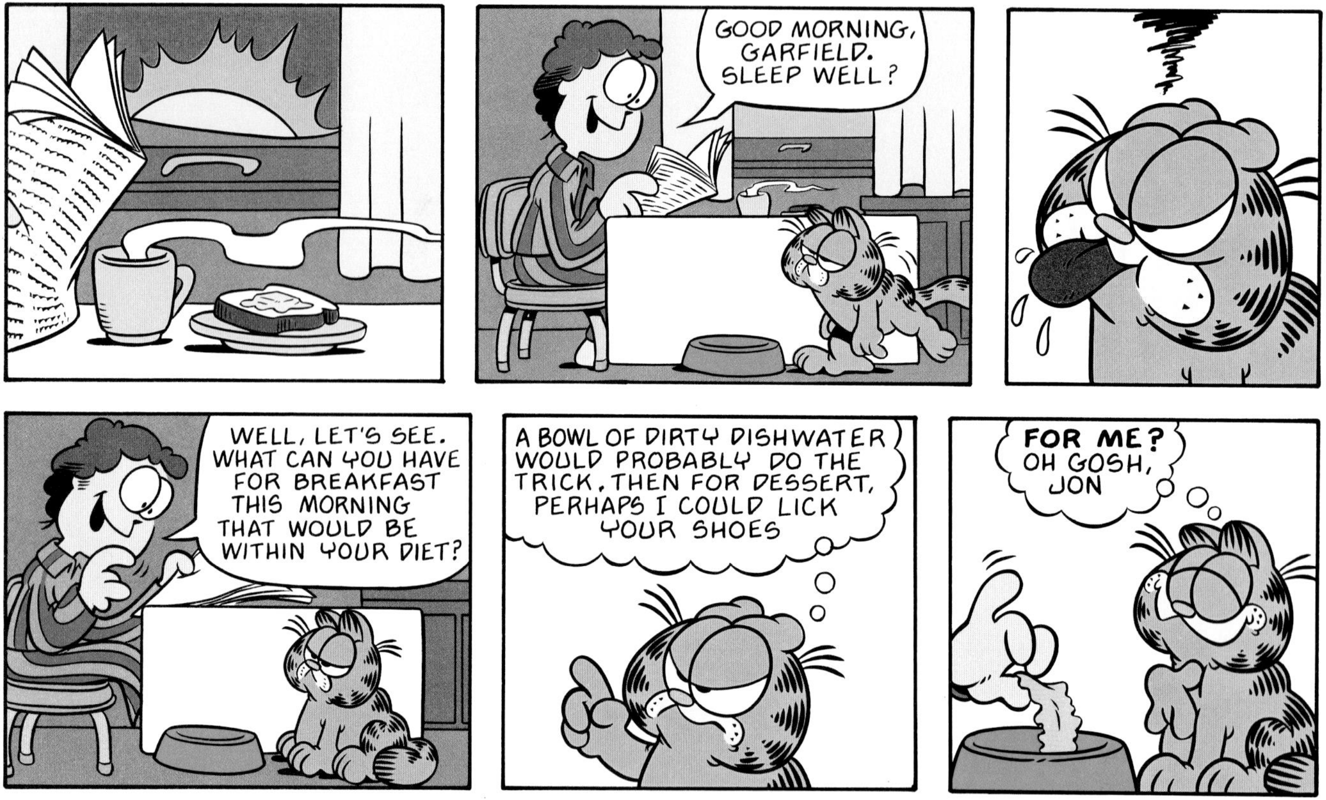
GOOD MORNING, GARFIELD. SLEEP WELL?
WELL, LET'S SEE. WHAT CAN YOU HAVE FOR BREAKFAST THIS MORNING THAT WOULD BE WITHIN YOUR DIET?
A BOWL OF DIRTY DISHWATER WOULD PROBABLY DO THE TRICK. THEN FOR DESSERT, PERHAPS I COULD LICK YOUR SHOES
FOR ME? OH GOSH, JON

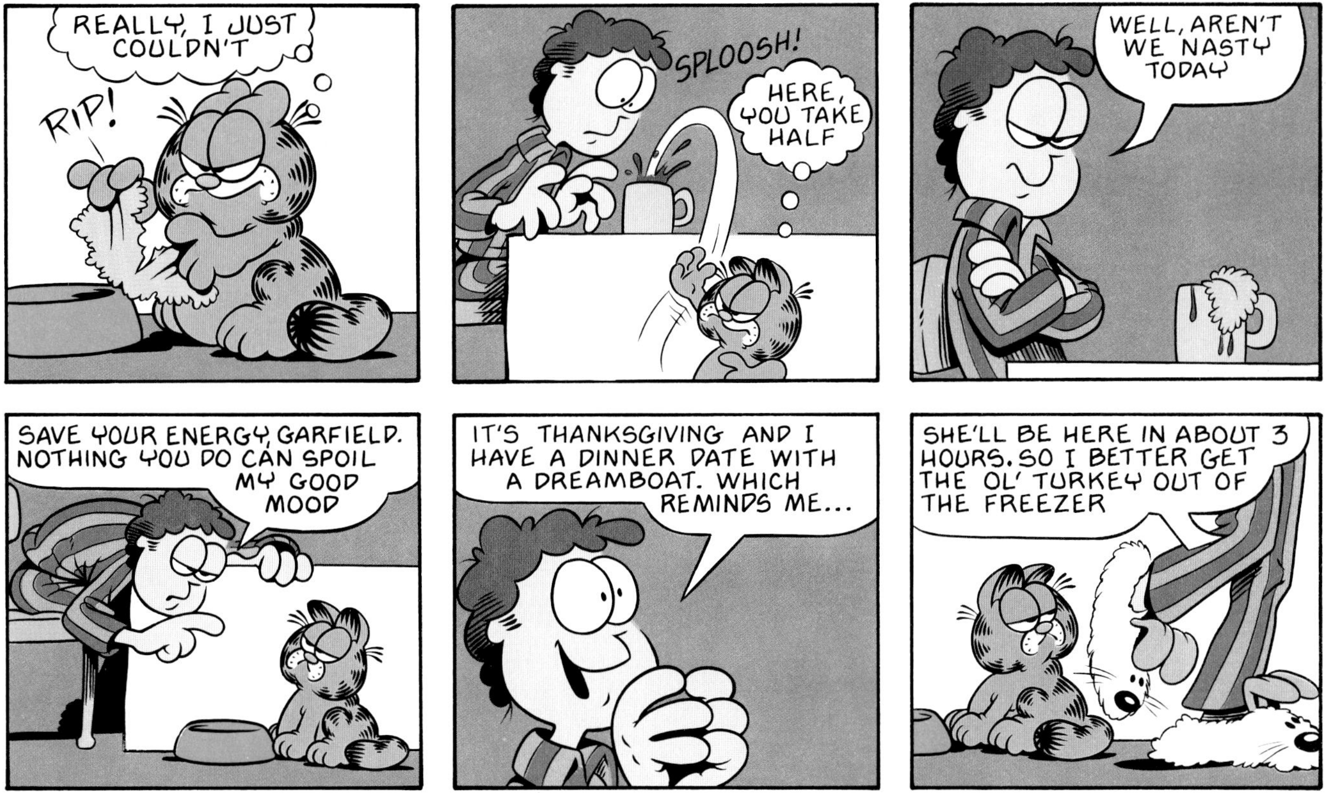
REALLY, I JUST COULDN'T
RIP!
SPLOOSH!
HERE, YOU TAKE HALF
WELL, AREN'T WE NASTY TODAY
SAVE YOUR ENERGY, GARFIELD. NOTHING YOU DO CAN SPOIL MY GOOD MOOD
IT'S THANKSGIVING AND I HAVE A DINNER DATE WITH A DREAMBOAT. WHICH REMINDS ME...
SHE'LL BE HERE IN ABOUT 3 HOURS. SO I BETTER GET THE OL' TURKEY OUT OF THE FREEZER

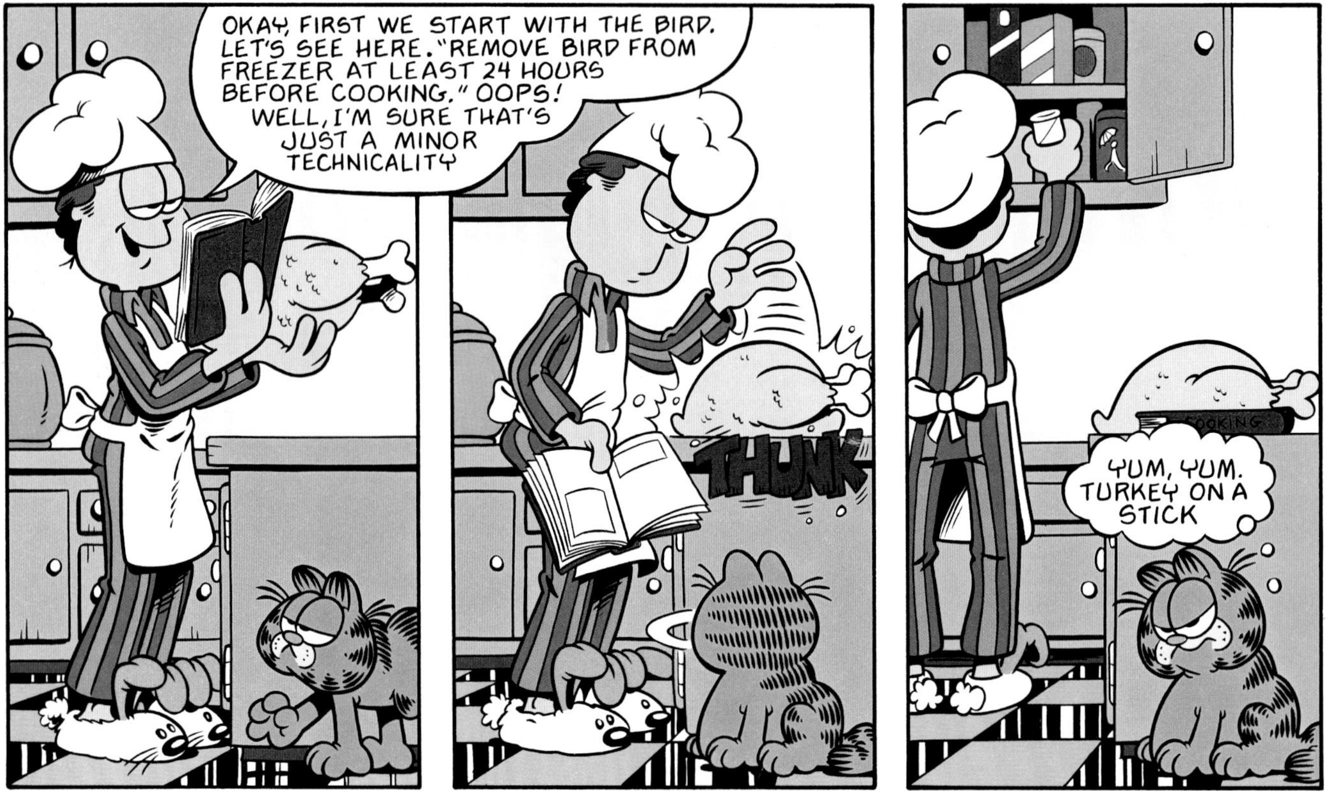
OKAY, FIRST WE START WITH THE BIRD. LET'S SEE HERE. "REMOVE BIRD FROM FREEZER AT LEAST 24 HOURS BEFORE COOKING." OOPS! WELL, I'M SURE THAT'S JUST A MINOR TECHNICALITY
THUNK
COOKING
YUM, YUM. TURKEY ON A STICK

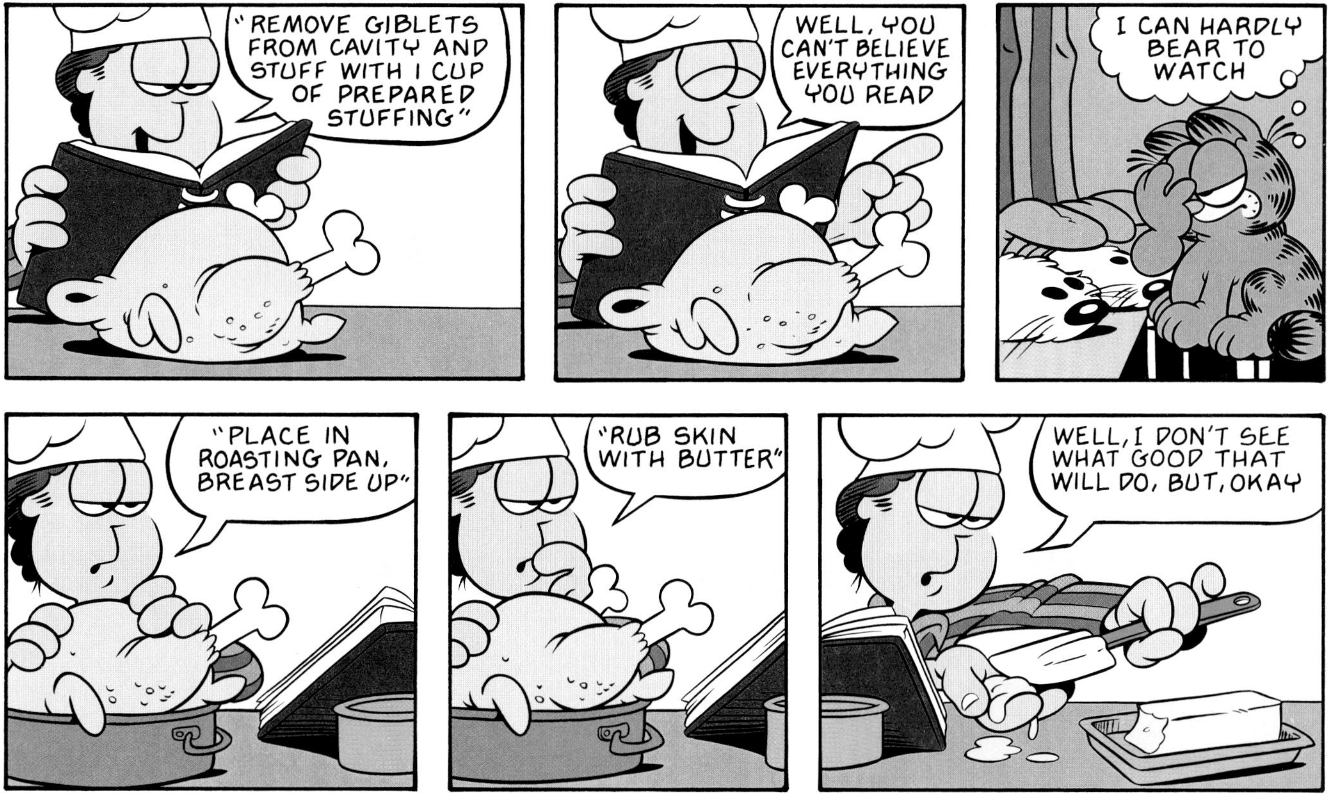
"REMOVE GIBLETS FROM CAVITY AND STUFF WITH 1 CUP OF PREPARED STUFFING"
WELL, YOU CAN'T BELIEVE EVERYTHING YOU READ
I CAN HARDLY BEAR TO WATCH
"PLACE IN ROASTING PAN, BREAST SIDE UP"
"RUB SKIN WITH BUTTER"
WELL, I DON'T SEE WHAT GOOD THAT WILL DO, BUT, OKAY

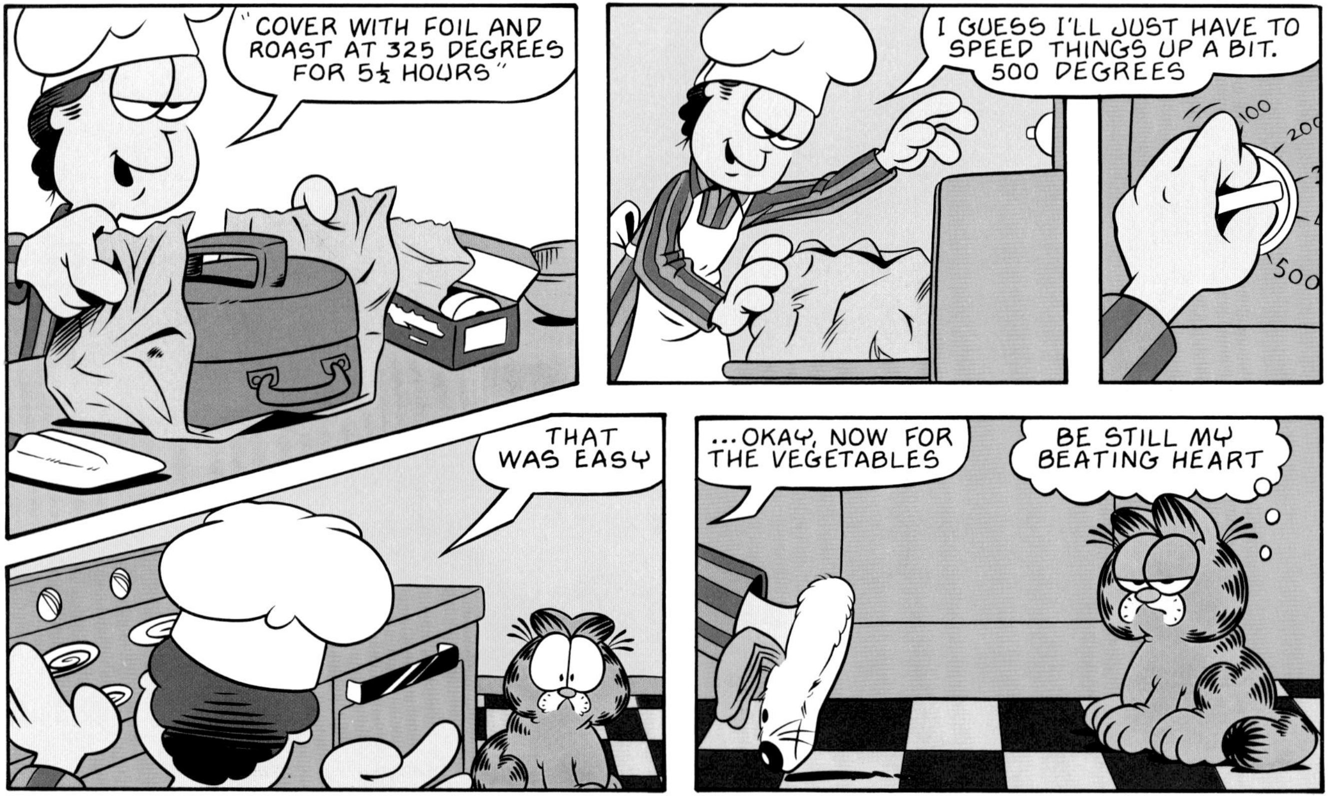
"COVER WITH FOIL AND ROAST AT 325 DEGREES FOR 5½ HOURS"
I GUESS I'LL JUST HAVE TO SPEED THINGS UP A BIT. 500 DEGREES
100
200
500
THAT WAS EASY
...OKAY, NOW FOR THE VEGETABLES
BE STILL MY BEATING HEART

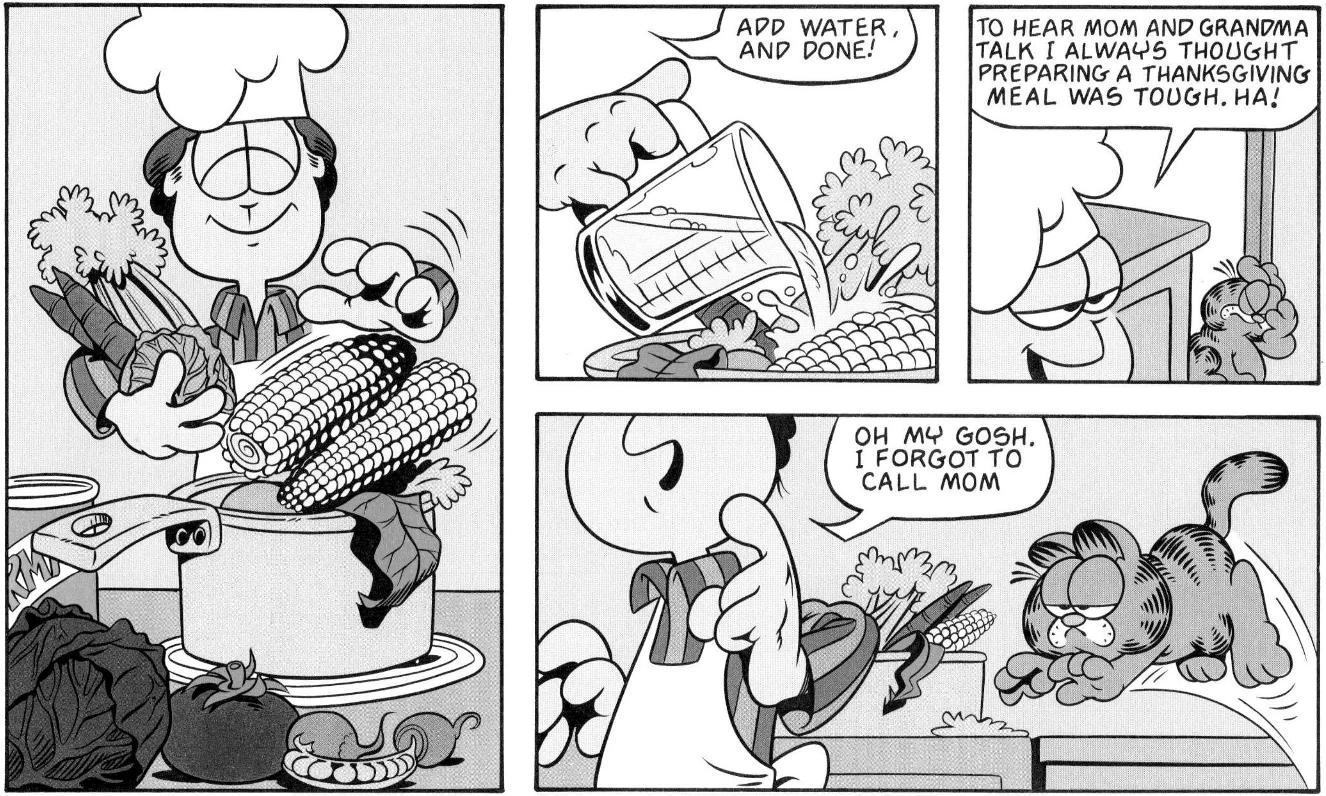
ADD WATER, AND DONE!
TO HEAR MOM AND GRANDMA TALK I ALWAYS THOUGHT PREPARING A THANKSGIVING MEAL WAS TOUGH. HA!
OH MY GOSH. I FORGOT TO CALL MOM

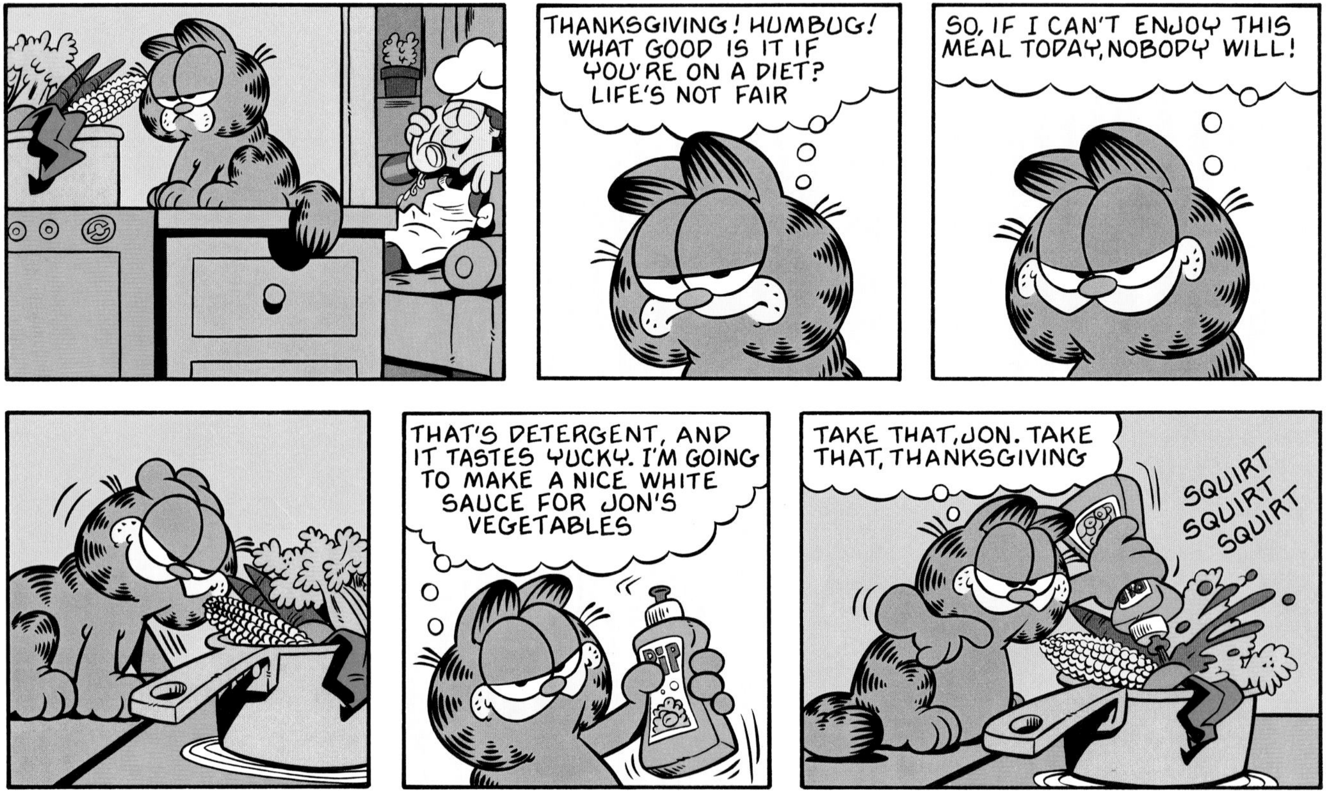
THANKSGIVING! HUMBUG! WHAT GOOD IS IT IF YOU'RE ON A DIET? LIFE'S NOT FAIR
SO, IF I CAN'T ENJOY THIS MEAL TODAY, NOBODY WILL!
THAT'S DETERGENT, AND IT TASTES YUCKY. I'M GOING TO MAKE A NICE WHITE SAUCE FOR JON'S VEGETABLES
DIP
TAKE THAT, JON. TAKE THAT, THANKSGIVING
SQUIRT
SQUIRT
SQUIRT

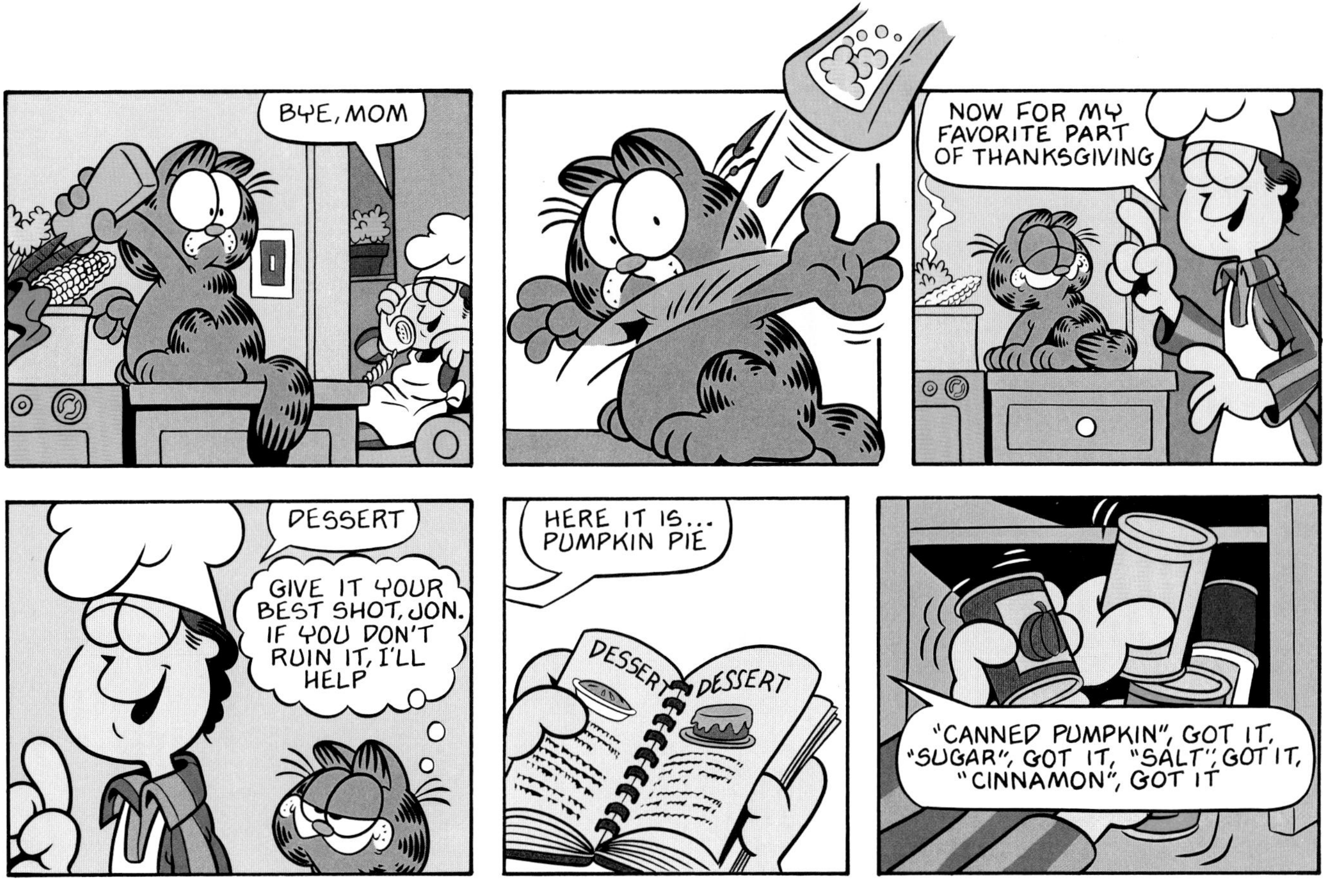
BYE, MOM
NOW FOR MY FAVORITE PART OF THANKSGIVING
DESSERT
GIVE IT YOUR BEST SHOT, JON. IF YOU DON'T RUIN IT, I'LL HELP
HERE IT IS... PUMPKIN PIE
DESSERT
DESSERT
"CANNED PUMPKIN", GOT IT, "SUGAR", GOT IT, "SALT", GOT IT, "CINNAMON", GOT IT

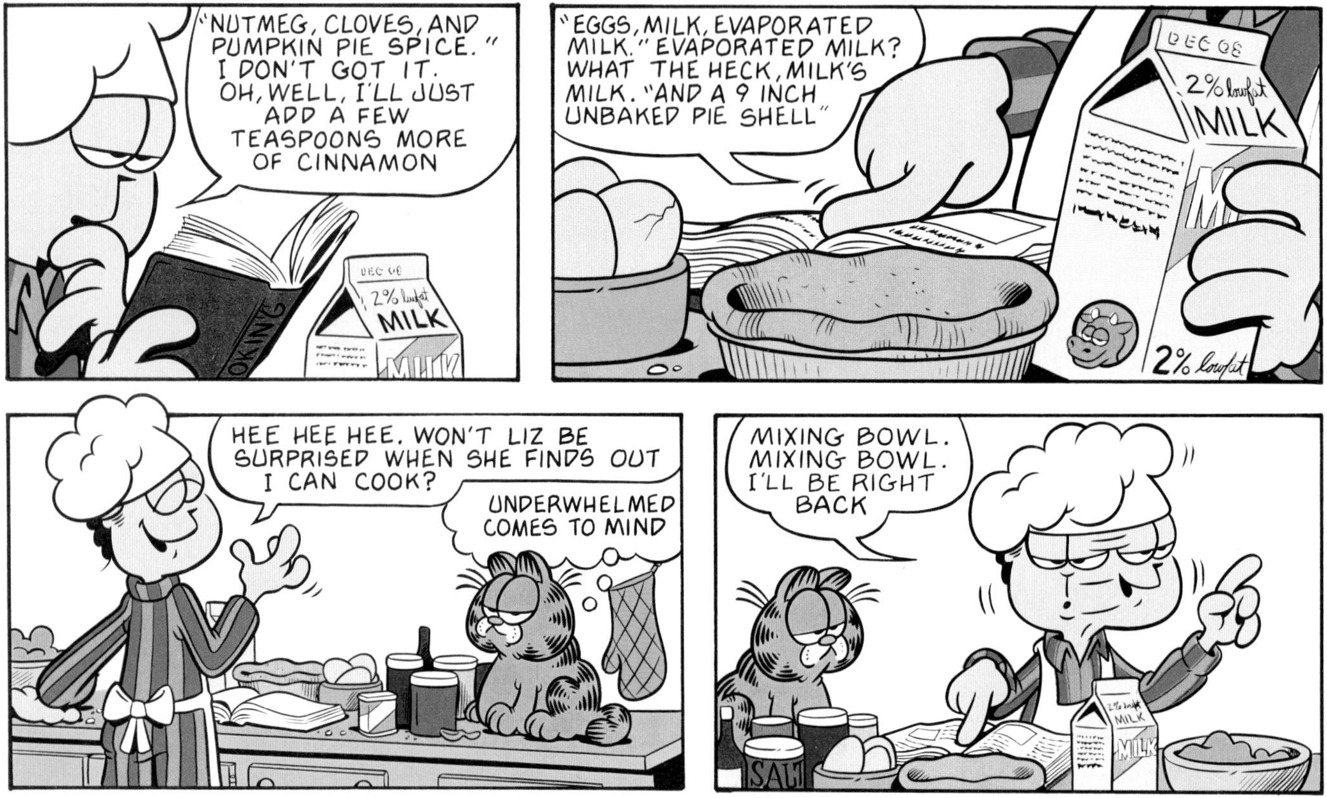
"NUTMEG, CLOVES, AND PUMPKIN PIE SPICE." I DON'T GOT IT. OH, WELL, I'LL JUST ADD A FEW TEASPOONS MORE OF CINNAMON
"EGGS, MILK, EVAPORATED MILK." EVAPORATED MILK? WHAT THE HECK, MILK'S MILK. "AND A 9 INCH UNBAKED PIE SHELL"
2% lowfat MILK
HEE HEE HEE. WON'T LIZ BE SURPRISED WHEN SHE FINDS OUT I CAN COOK?
UNDERWHELMED COMES TO MIND
MIXING BOWL. MIXING BOWL. I'LL BE RIGHT BACK

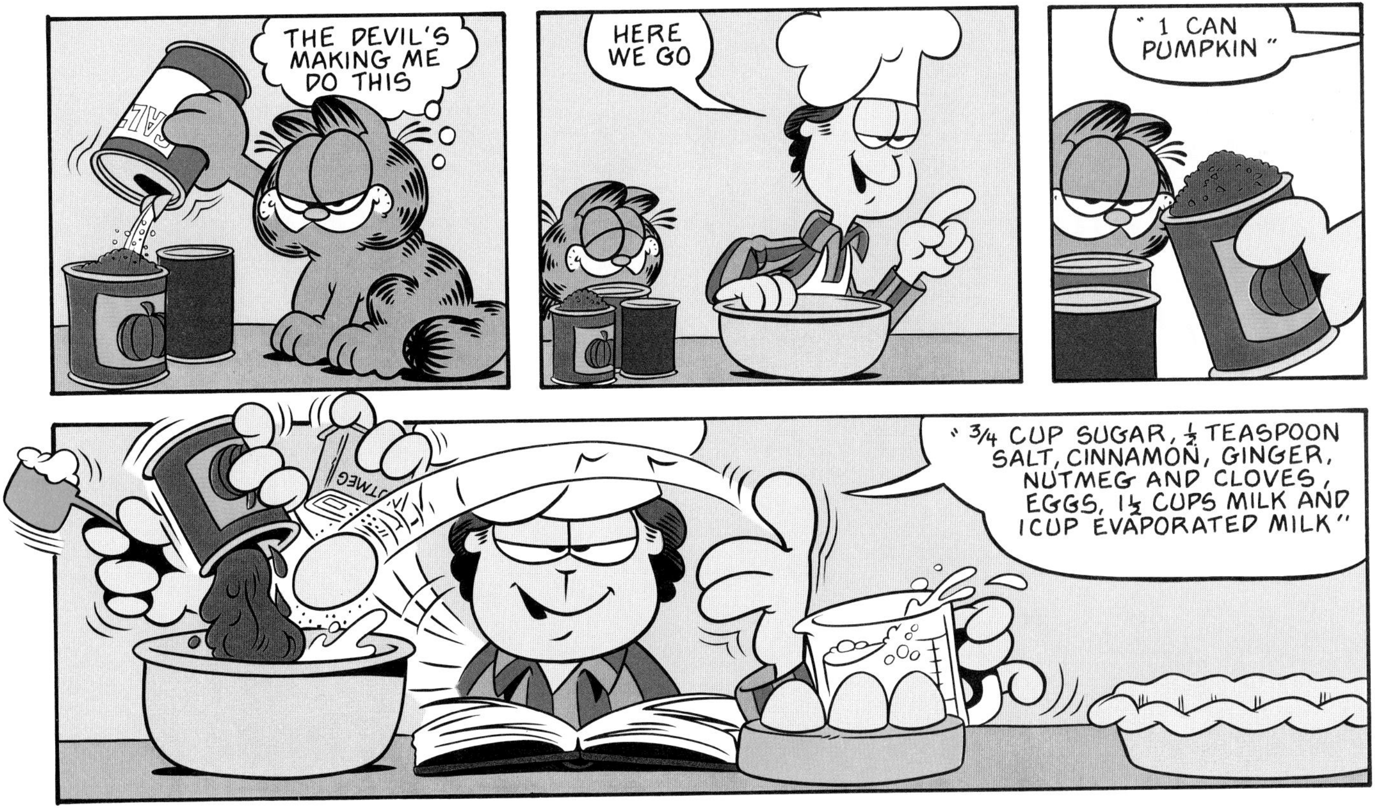
THE DEVIL'S MAKING ME DO THIS
HERE WE GO
"1 CAN PUMPKIN"
"3/4 CUP SUGAR, 1/2 TEASPOON SALT, CINNAMON, GINGER, NUTMEG AND CLOVES, EGGS, 1 1/2 CUPS MILK AND 1 CUP EVAPORATED MILK"

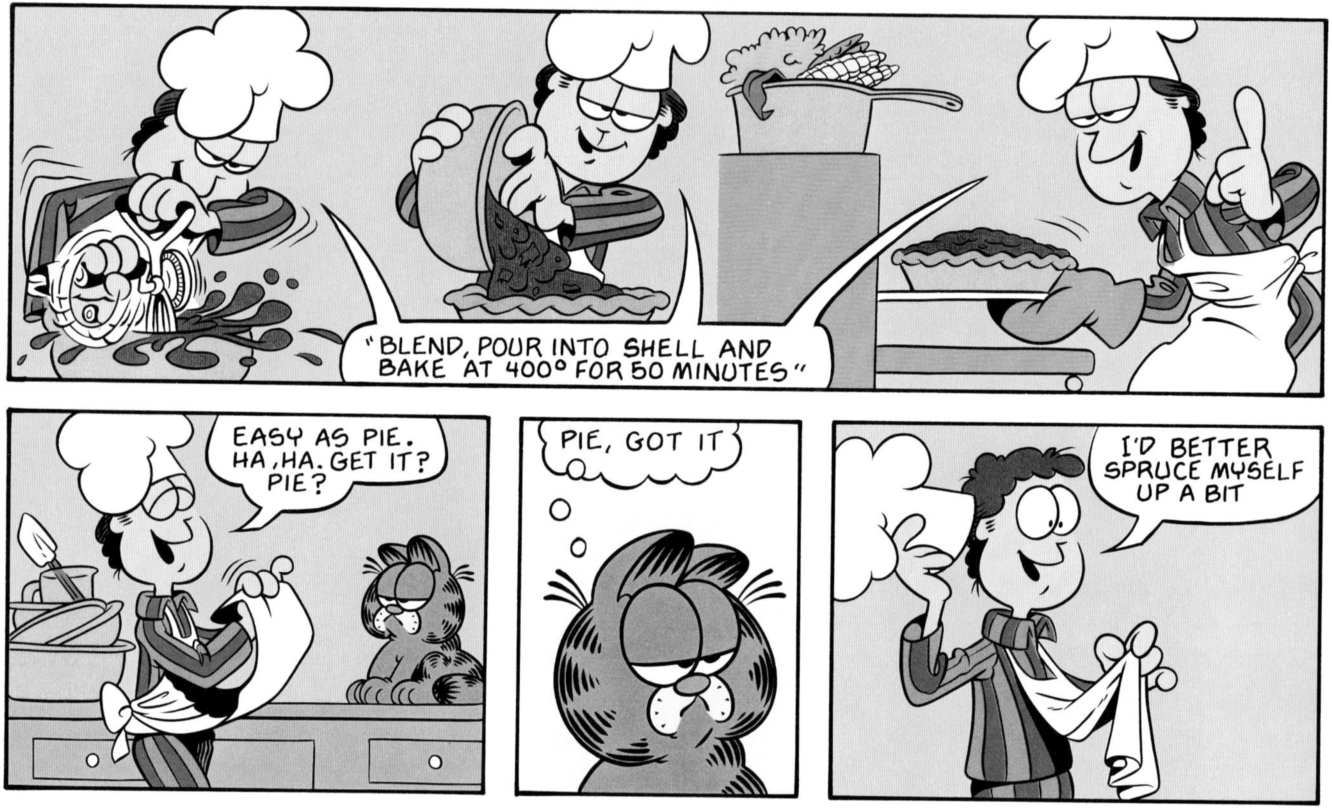
"BLEND, POUR INTO SHELL AND BAKE AT 400° FOR 50 MINUTES"
EASY AS PIE. HA, HA. GET IT? PIE?
PIE, GOT IT
I'D BETTER SPRUCE MYSELF UP A BIT

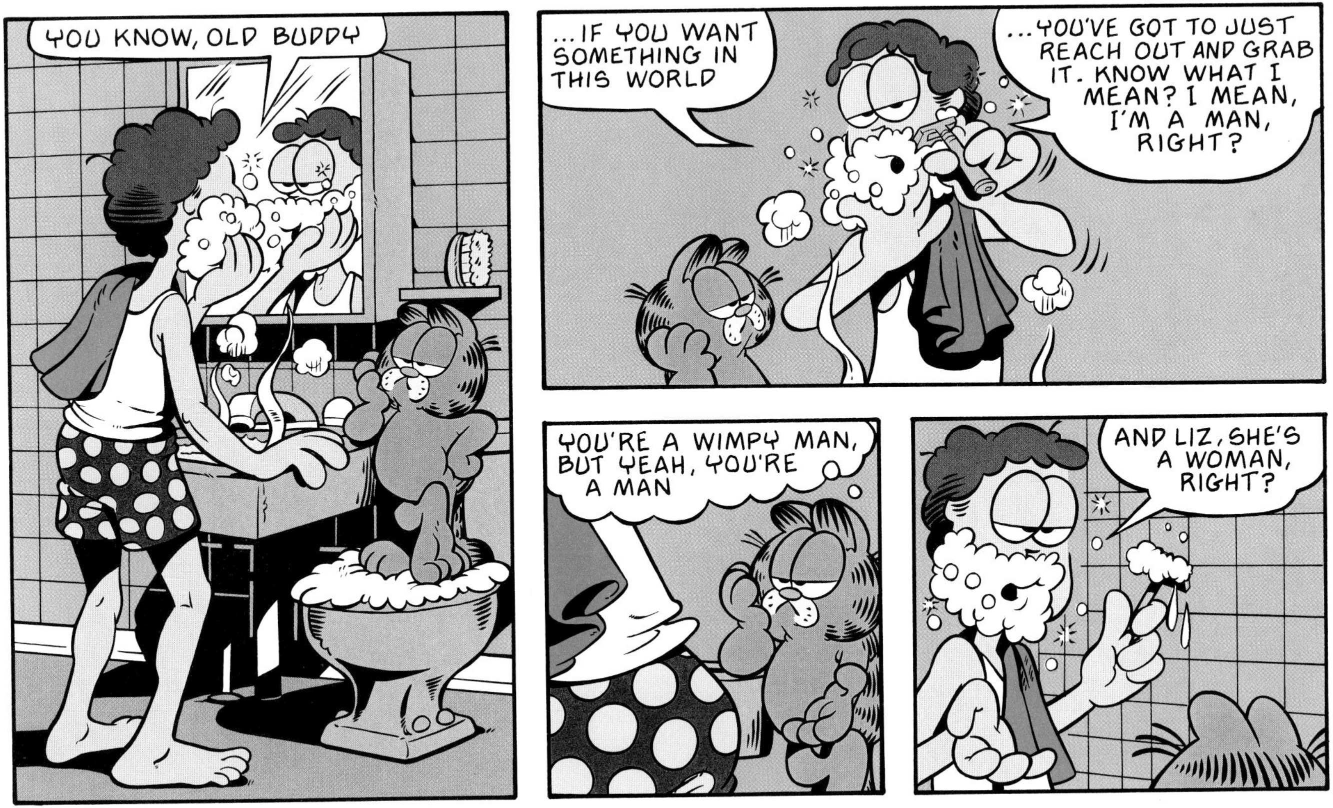
YOU KNOW, OLD BUDDY
...IF YOU WANT SOMETHING IN THIS WORLD
...YOU'VE GOT TO JUST REACH OUT AND GRAB IT. KNOW WHAT I MEAN? I MEAN, I'M A MAN, RIGHT?
YOU'RE A WIMPY MAN, BUT YEAH, YOU'RE A MAN
AND LIZ, SHE'S A WOMAN, RIGHT?

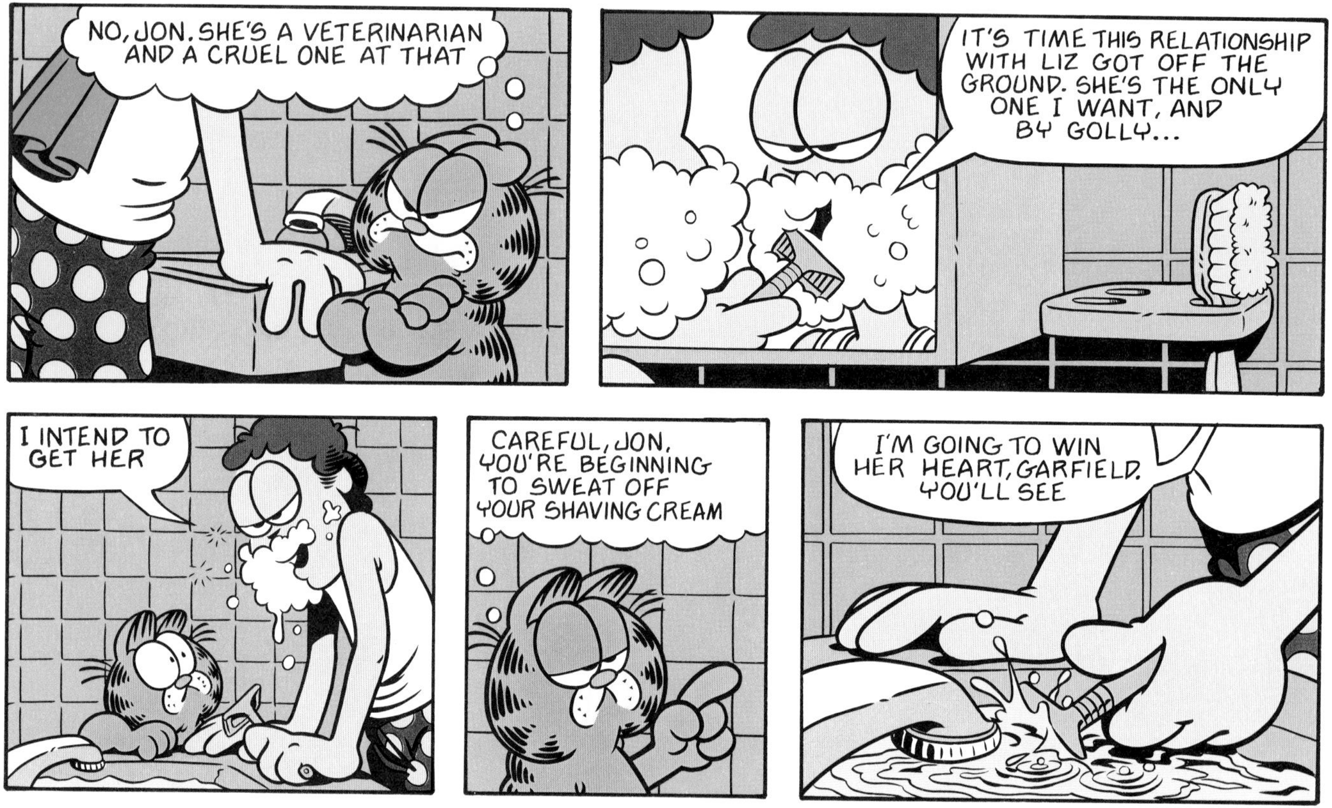
NO, JON. SHE'S A VETERINARIAN AND A CRUEL ONE AT THAT
IT'S TIME THIS RELATIONSHIP WITH LIZ GOT OFF THE GROUND. SHE'S THE ONLY ONE I WANT, AND BY GOLLY...
I INTEND TO GET HER
CAREFUL, JON, YOU'RE BEGINNING TO SWEAT OFF YOUR SHAVING CREAM
I'M GOING TO WIN HER HEART, GARFIELD. YOU'LL SEE

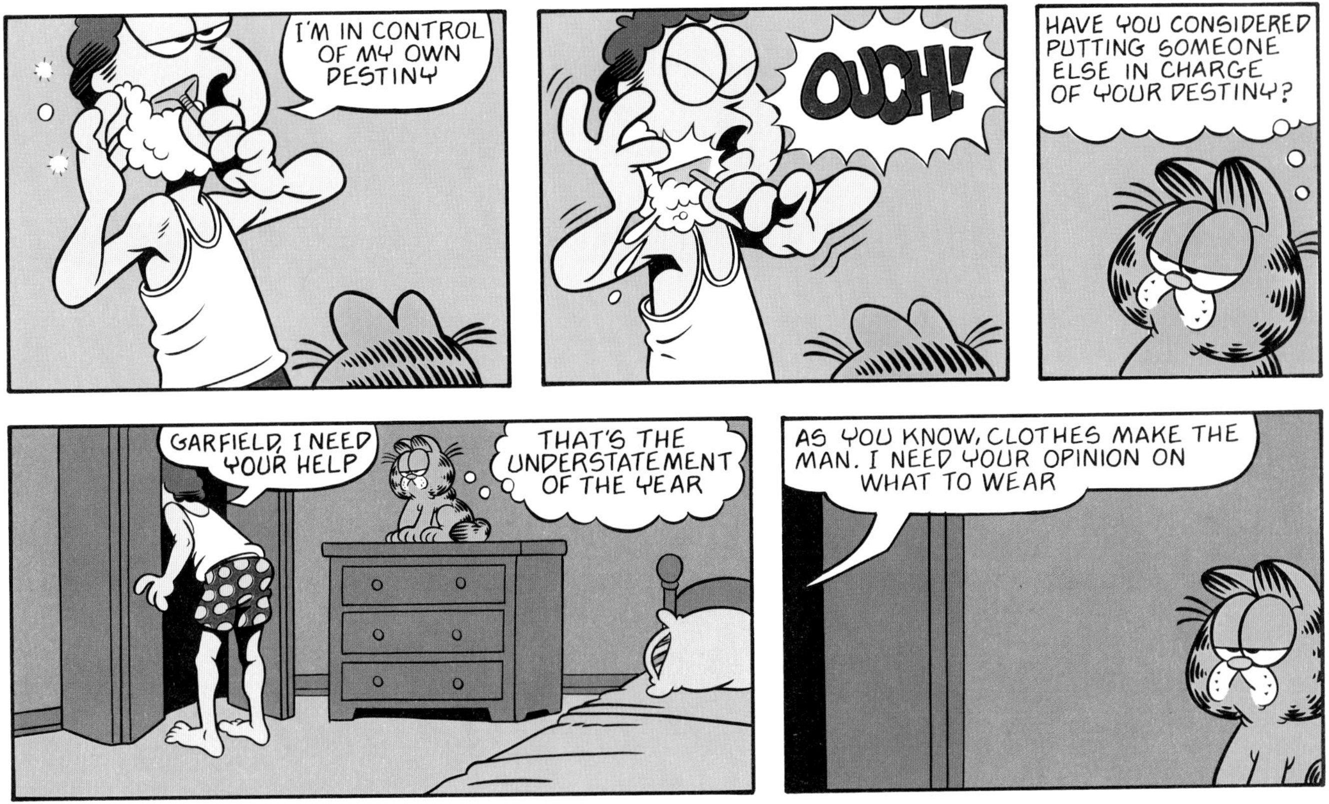
I'M IN CONTROL OF MY OWN DESTINY
OUCH!
HAVE YOU CONSIDERED PUTTING SOMEONE ELSE IN CHARGE OF YOUR DESTINY?
GARFIELD, I NEED YOUR HELP
THAT'S THE UNDERSTATEMENT OF THE YEAR
AS YOU KNOW, CLOTHES MAKE THE MAN. I NEED YOUR OPINION ON WHAT TO WEAR

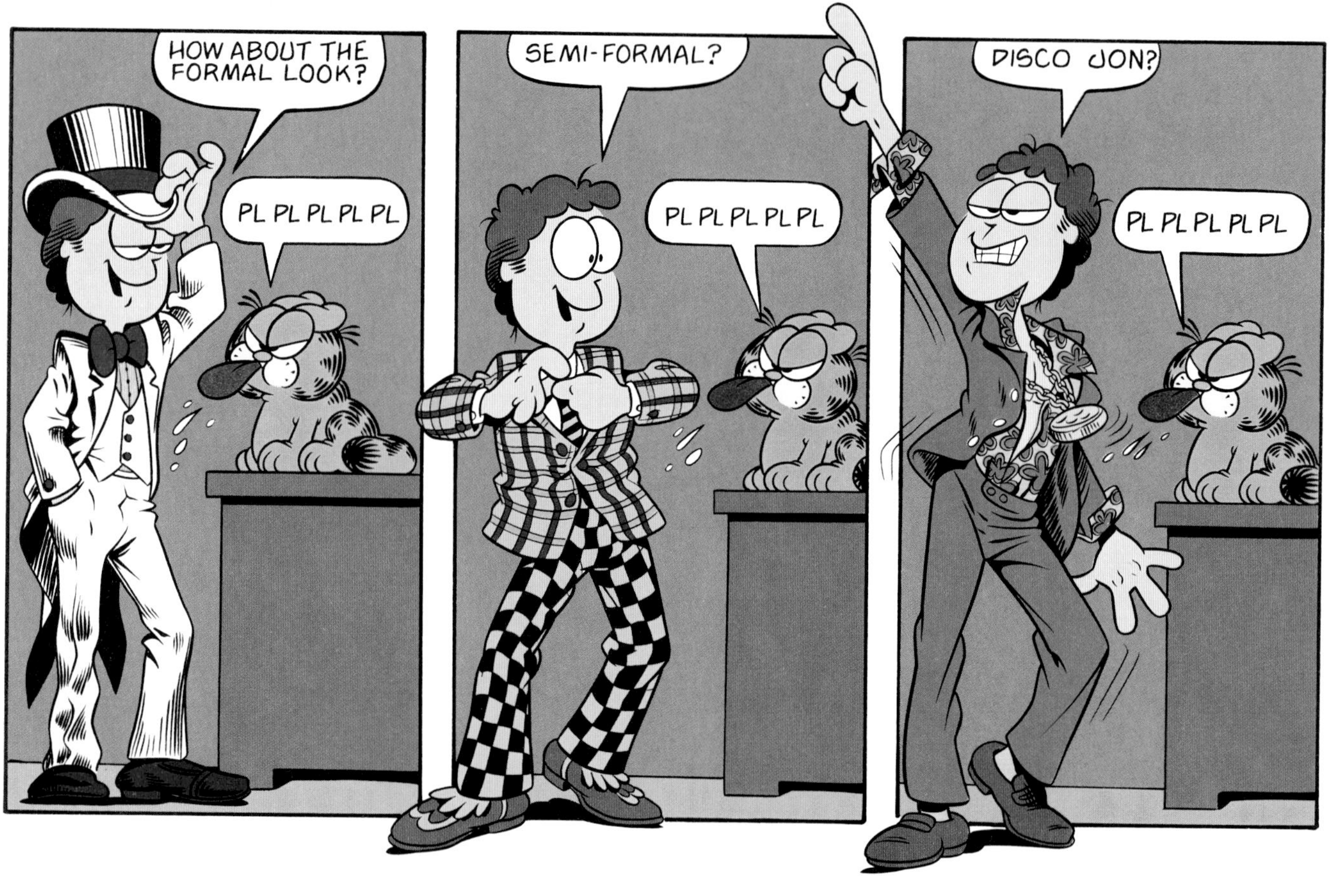
HOW ABOUT THE FORMAL LOOK?
PL PL PL PL PL
SEMI-FORMAL?
PL PL PL PL PL
DISCO JON?
PL PL PL PL PL

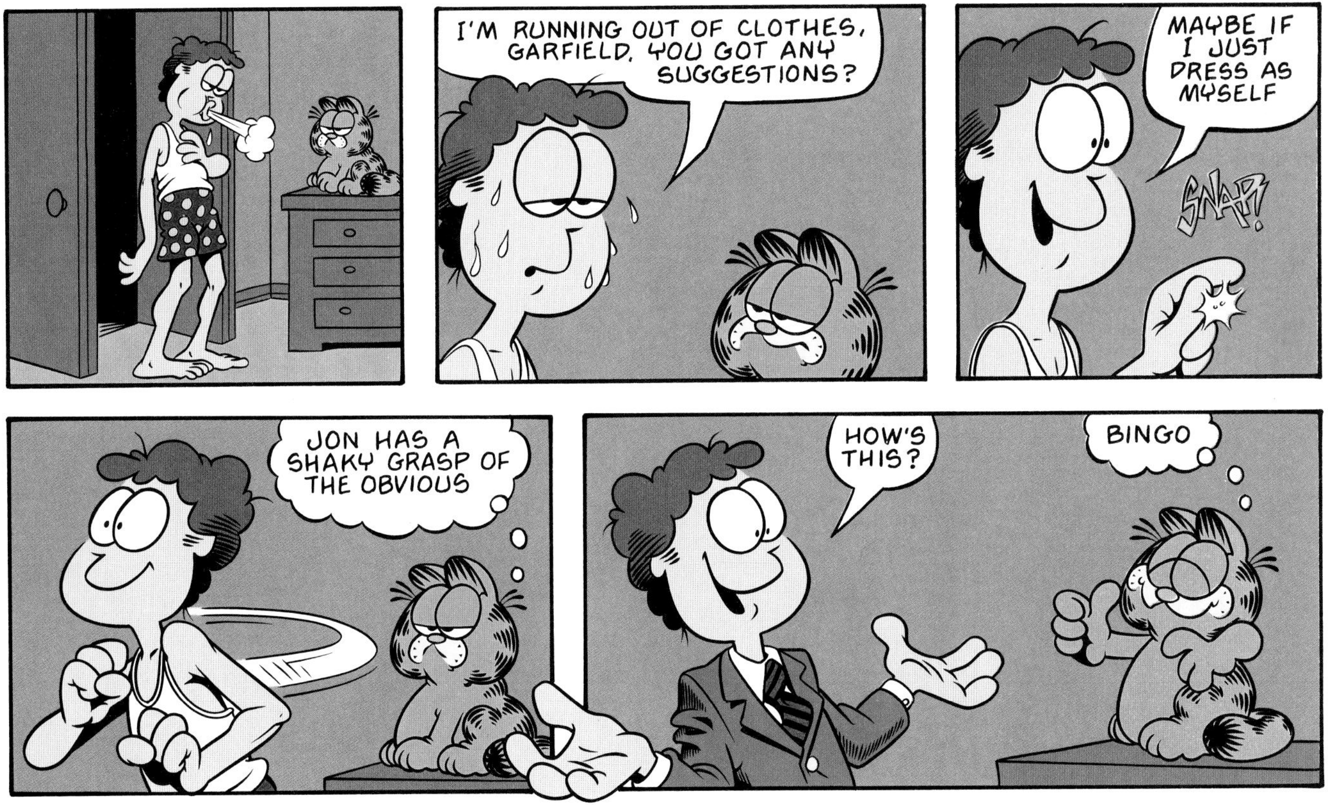
I'M RUNNING OUT OF CLOTHES, GARFIELD. YOU GOT ANY SUGGESTIONS?
MAYBE IF I JUST DRESS AS MYSELF
SNAP!
JON HAS A SHAKY GRASP OF THE OBVIOUS
HOW'S THIS?
BINGO

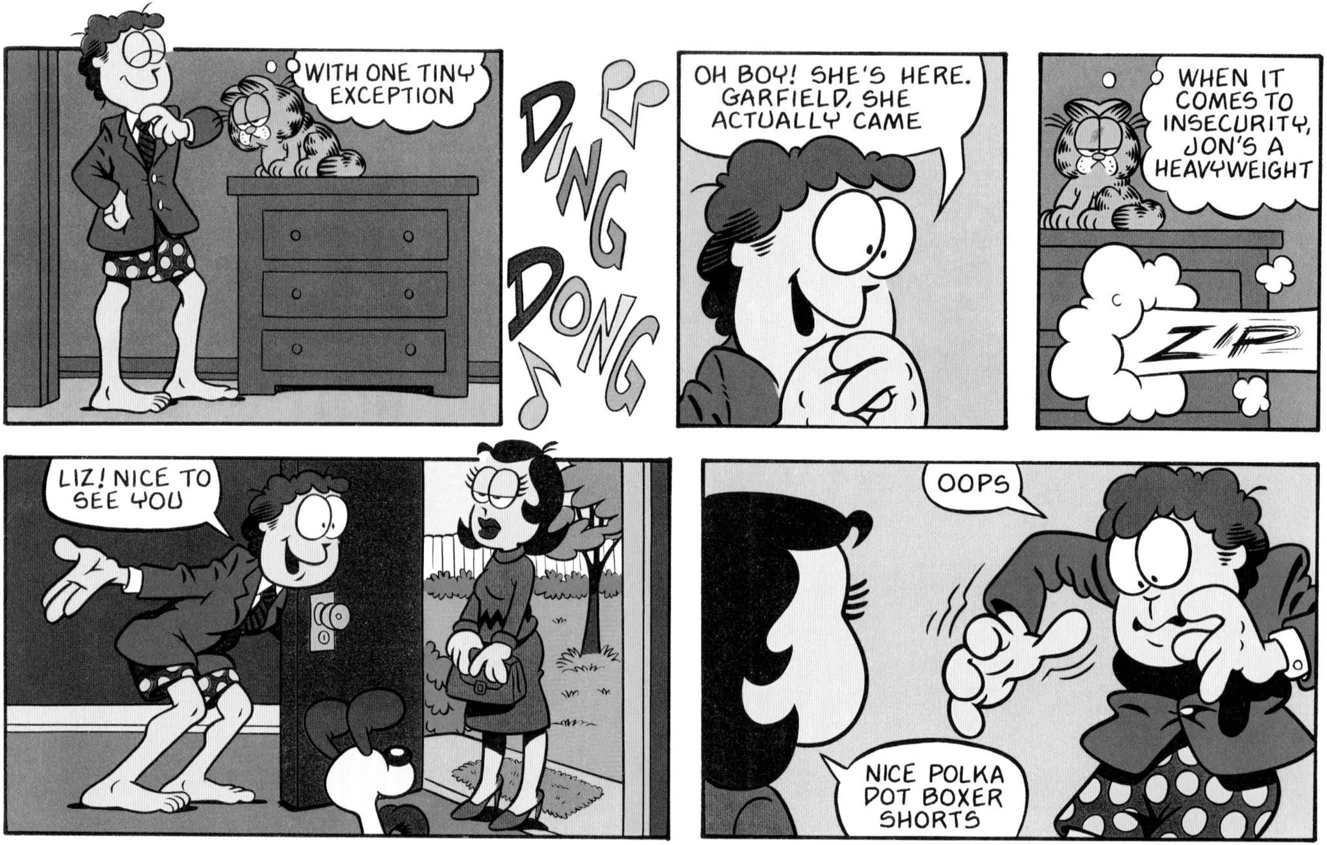
WITH ONE TINY EXCEPTION
DING DONG
OH BOY! SHE'S HERE. GARFIELD, SHE ACTUALLY CAME
WHEN IT COMES TO INSECURITY, JON'S A HEAVYWEIGHT
ZIP
LIZ! NICE TO SEE YOU
OOPS
NICE POLKA DOT BOXER SHORTS

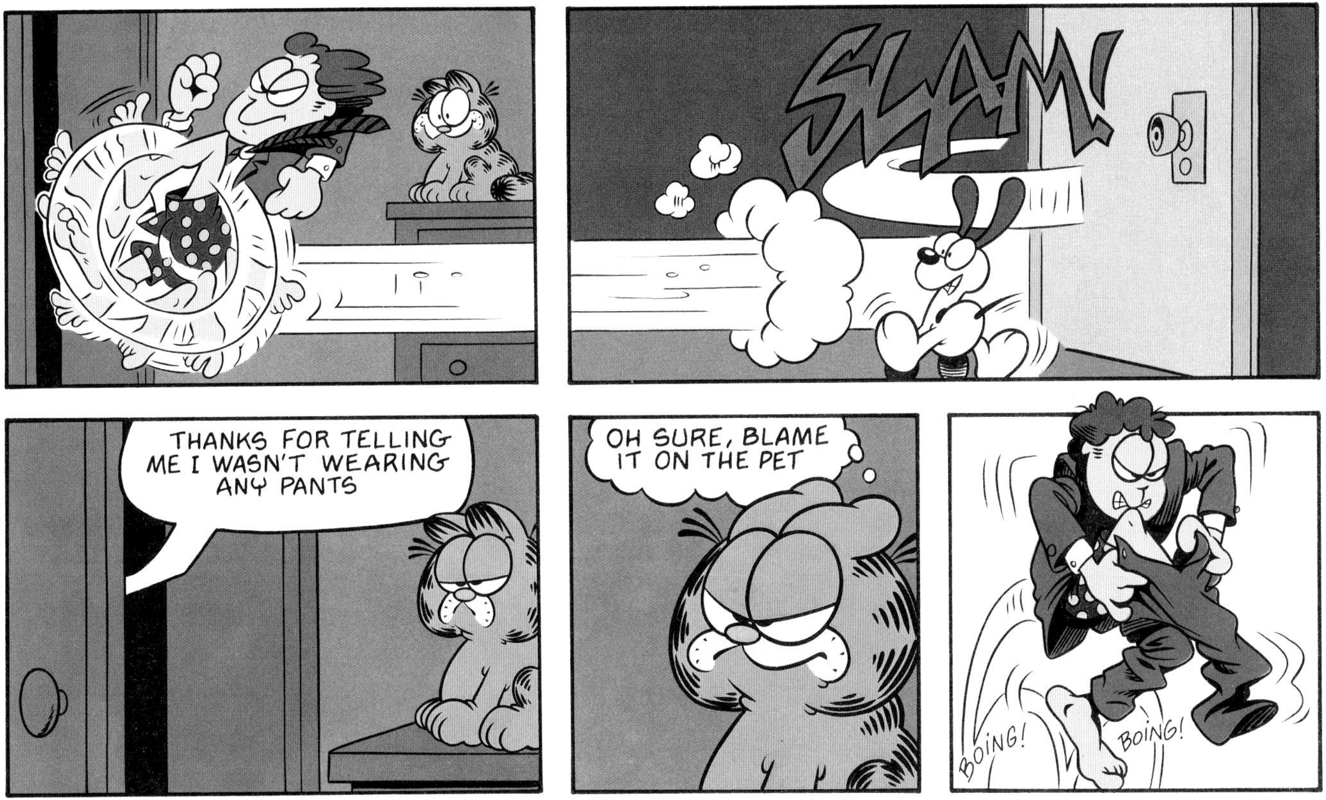
SLAM!
THANKS FOR TELLING ME I WASN'T WEARING ANY PANTS
OH SURE, BLAME IT ON THE PET
BOING!
BOING!

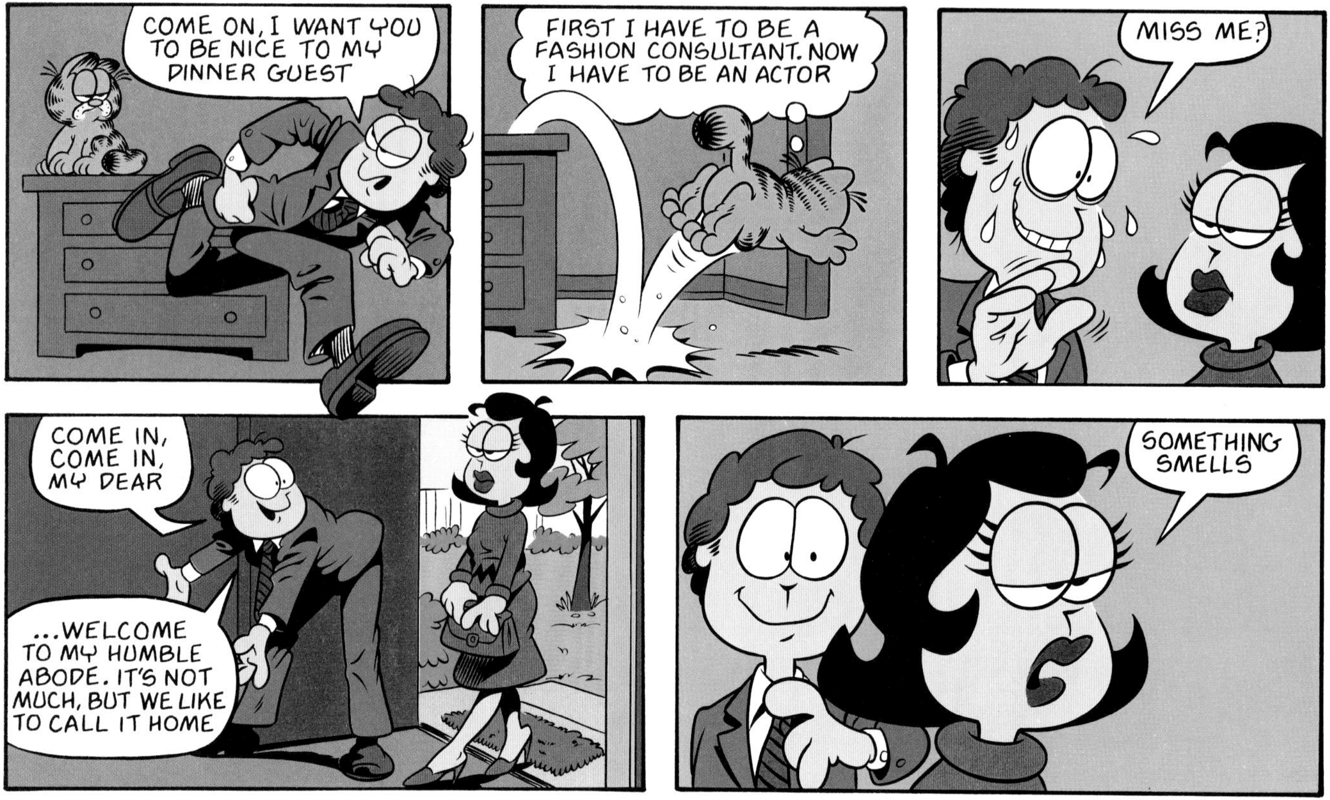
COME ON, I WANT YOU TO BE NICE TO MY DINNER GUEST
FIRST I HAVE TO BE A FASHION CONSULTANT. NOW I HAVE TO BE AN ACTOR
MISS ME?
COME IN, COME IN, MY DEAR
...WELCOME TO MY HUMBLE ABODE. IT'S NOT MUCH, BUT WE LIKE TO CALL IT HOME
SOMETHING SMELLS

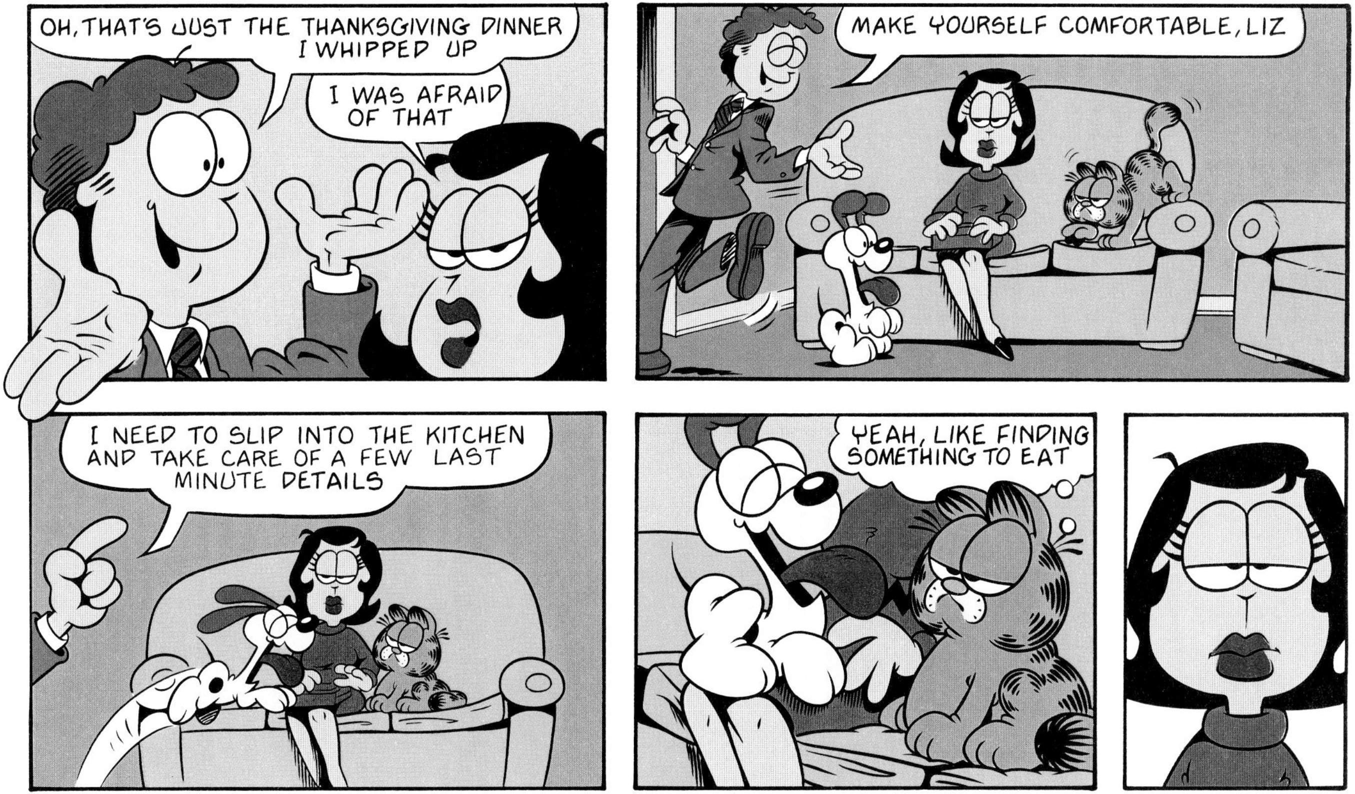
OH, THAT'S JUST THE THANKSGIVING DINNER I WHIPPED UP
I WAS AFRAID OF THAT
MAKE YOURSELF COMFORTABLE, LIZ
I NEED TO SLIP INTO THE KITCHEN AND TAKE CARE OF A FEW LAST MINUTE DETAILS
YEAH, LIKE FINDING SOMETHING TO EAT

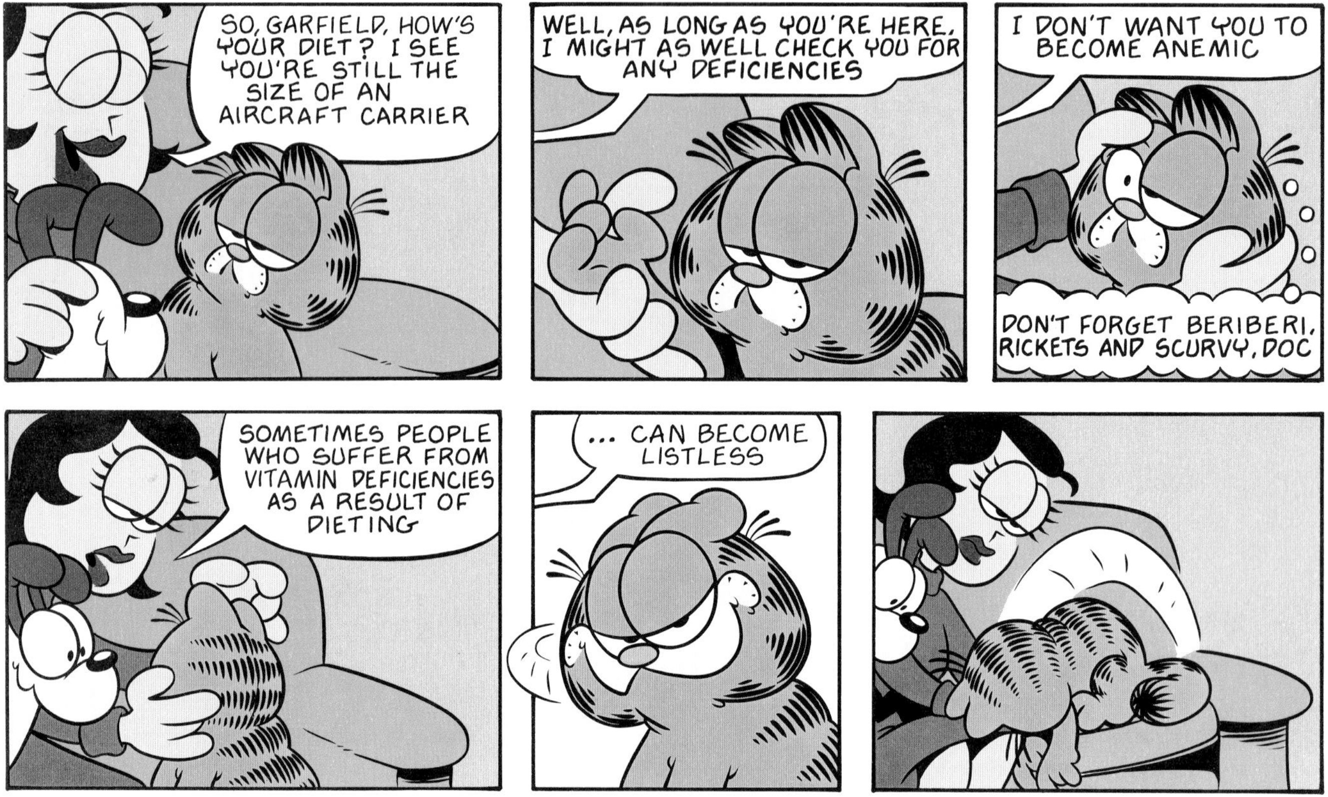
SO, GARFIELD, HOW'S YOUR DIET? I SEE YOU'RE STILL THE SIZE OF AN AIRCRAFT CARRIER
WELL, AS LONG AS YOU'RE HERE, I MIGHT AS WELL CHECK YOU FOR ANY DEFICIENCIES
I DON'T WANT YOU TO BECOME ANEMIC
DON'T FORGET BERIBERI, RICKETS AND SCURVY, DOC
SOMETIMES PEOPLE WHO SUFFER FROM VITAMIN DEFICIENCIES AS A RESULT OF DIETING
... CAN BECOME LISTLESS

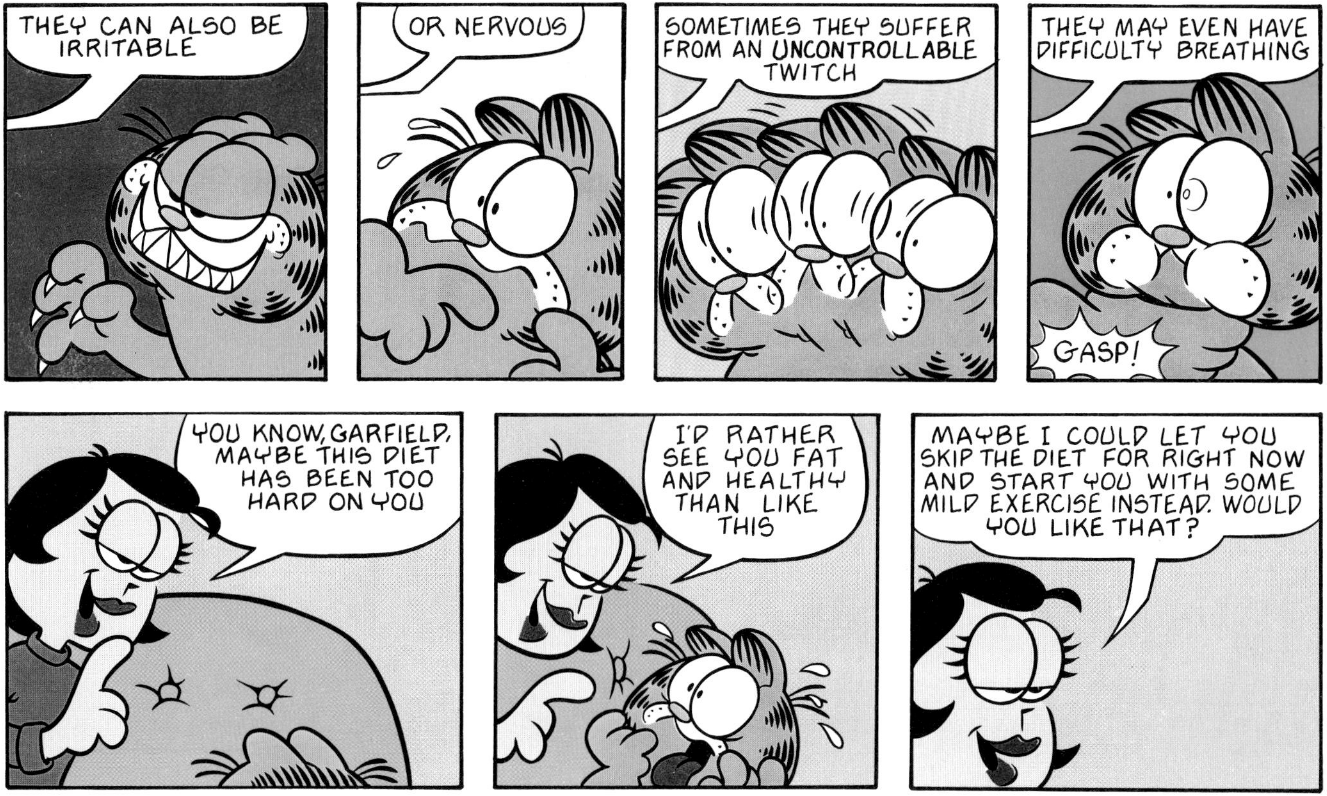
THEY CAN ALSO BE IRRITABLE
OR NERVOUS
SOMETIMES THEY SUFFER FROM AN UNCONTROLLABLE TWITCH
THEY MAY EVEN HAVE DIFFICULTY BREATHING
GASP!
YOU KNOW, GARFIELD, MAYBE THIS DIET HAS BEEN TOO HARD ON YOU
I'D RATHER SEE YOU FAT AND HEALTHY THAN LIKE THIS
MAYBE I COULD LET YOU SKIP THE DIET FOR RIGHT NOW AND START YOU WITH SOME MILD EXERCISE INSTEAD. WOULD YOU LIKE THAT?

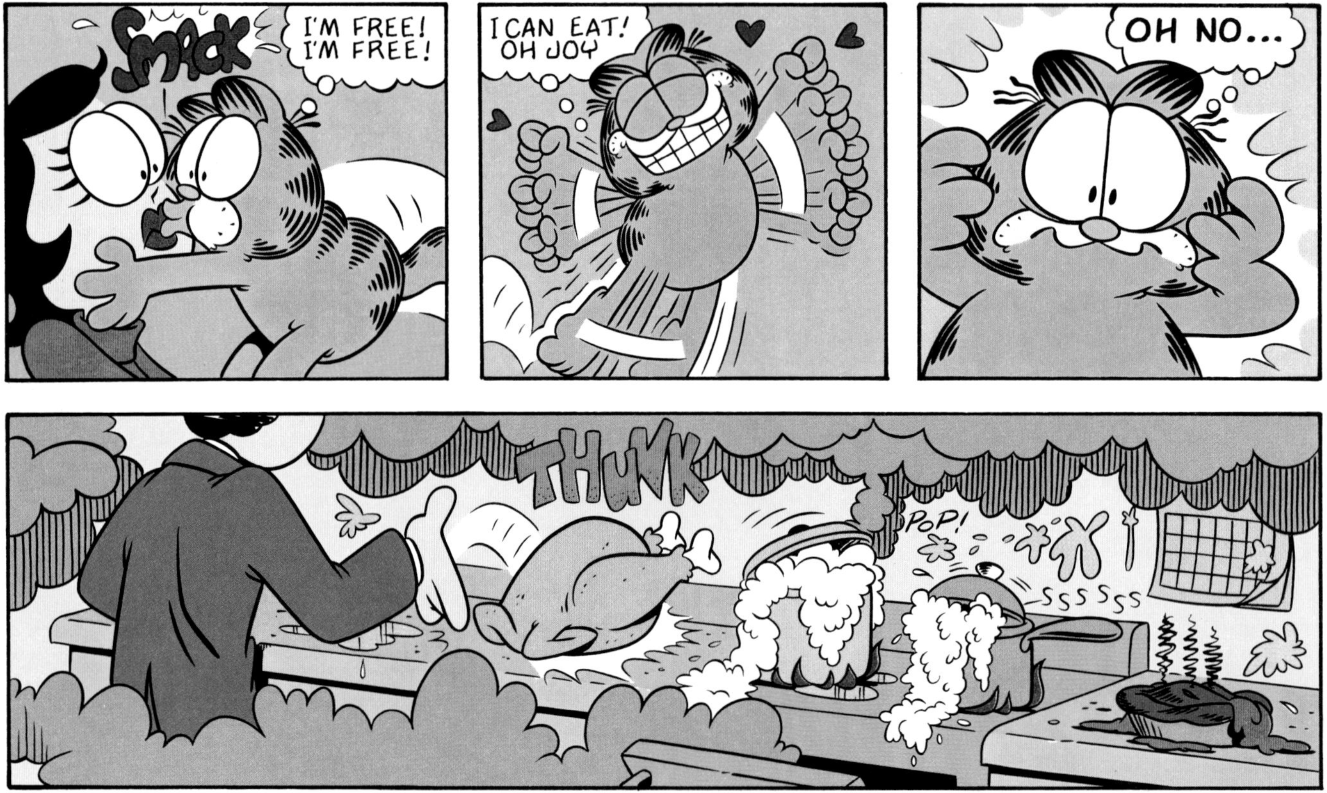
SMACK
I'M FREE! I'M FREE!
I CAN EAT! OH JOY
OH NO...
THUNK
POP!
SSSSSS

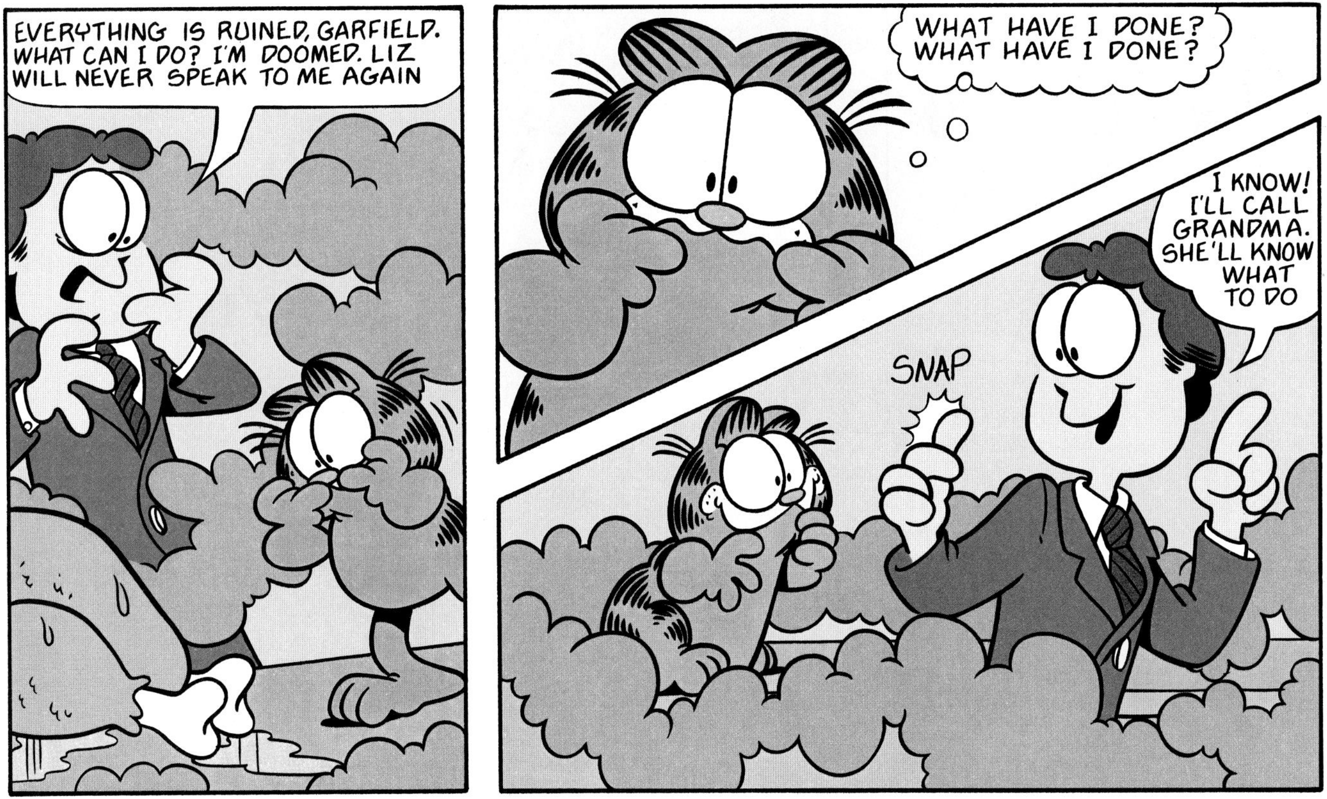
EVERYTHING IS RUINED, GARFIELD. WHAT CAN I DO? I'M DOOMED. LIZ WILL NEVER SPEAK TO ME AGAIN
WHAT HAVE I DONE? WHAT HAVE I DONE?
SNAP
I KNOW! I'LL CALL GRANDMA. SHE'LL KNOW WHAT TO DO

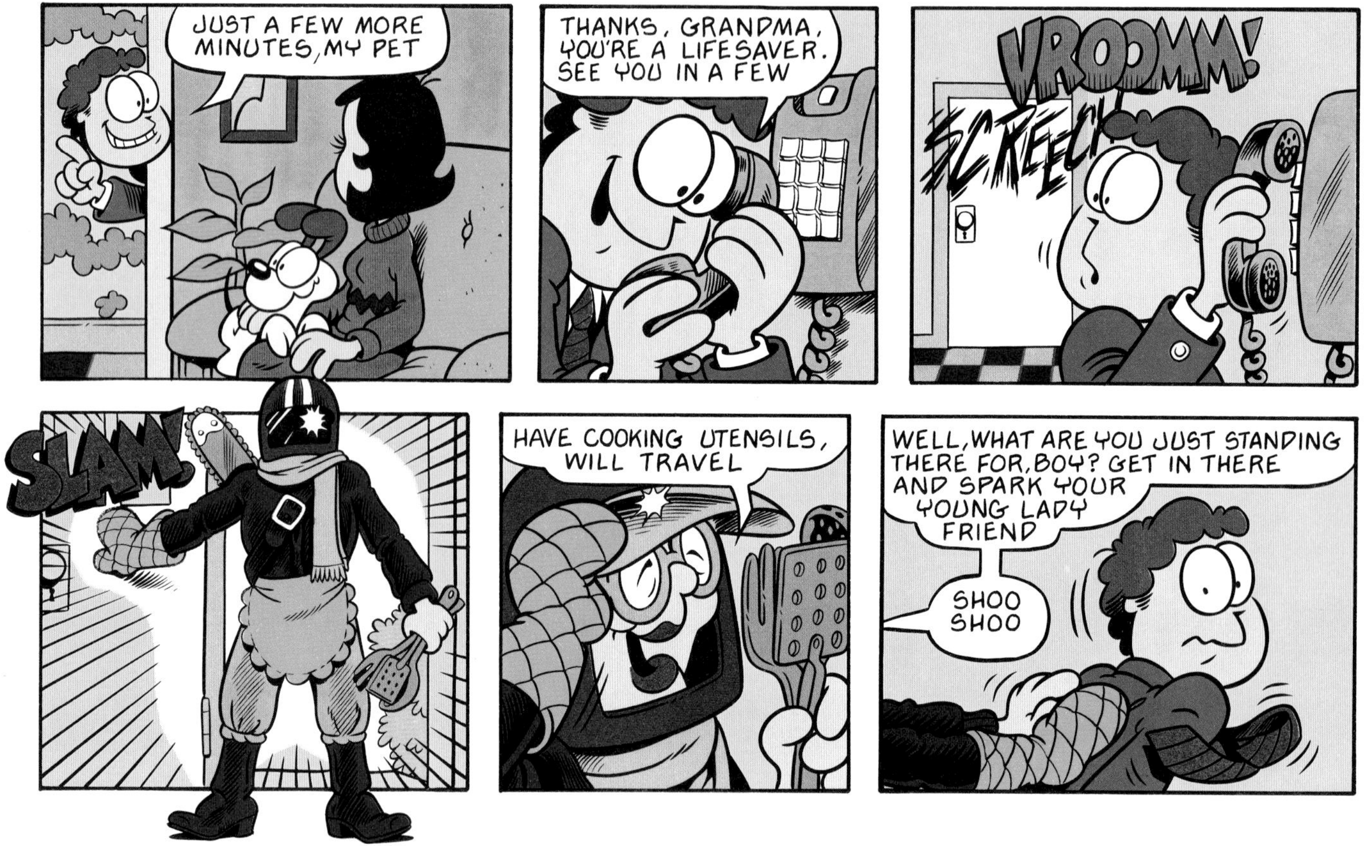
JUST A FEW MORE MINUTES, MY PET
THANKS, GRANDMA, YOU'RE A LIFESAVER. SEE YOU IN A FEW
VROOMM!
SCREECH
SLAM!
HAVE COOKING UTENSILS, WILL TRAVEL
WELL, WHAT ARE YOU JUST STANDING THERE FOR, BOY? GET IN THERE AND SPARK YOUR YOUNG LADY FRIEND
SHOO SHOO

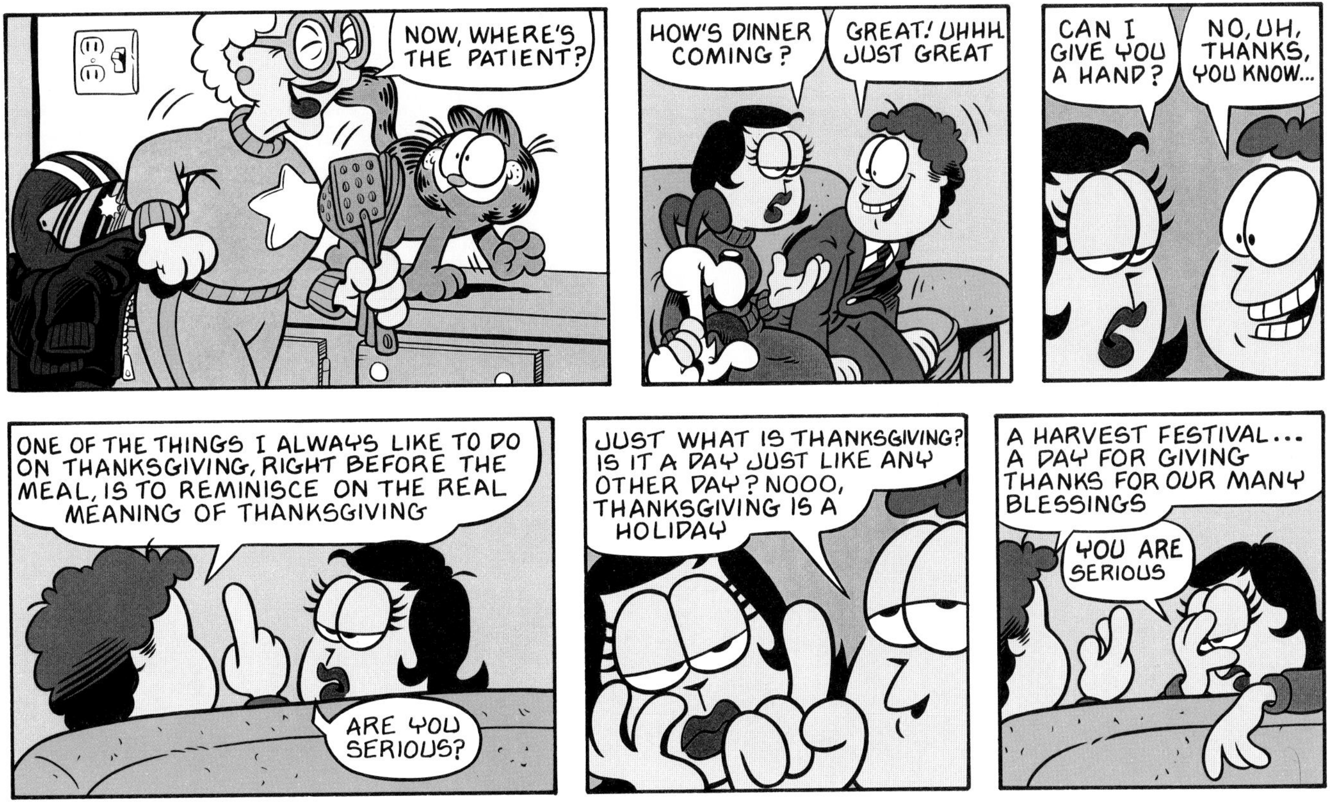
NOW, WHERE'S THE PATIENT?
HOW'S DINNER COMING?
GREAT! UHHH. JUST GREAT
CAN I GIVE YOU A HAND?
NO, UH, THANKS, YOU KNOW...
ONE OF THE THINGS I ALWAYS LIKE TO DO ON THANKSGIVING, RIGHT BEFORE THE MEAL, IS TO REMINISCE ON THE REAL MEANING OF THANKSGIVING
ARE YOU SERIOUS?
JUST WHAT IS THANKSGIVING? IS IT A DAY JUST LIKE ANY OTHER DAY? NOOO, THANKSGIVING IS A HOLIDAY
A HARVEST FESTIVAL... A DAY FOR GIVING THANKS FOR OUR MANY BLESSINGS
YOU ARE SERIOUS

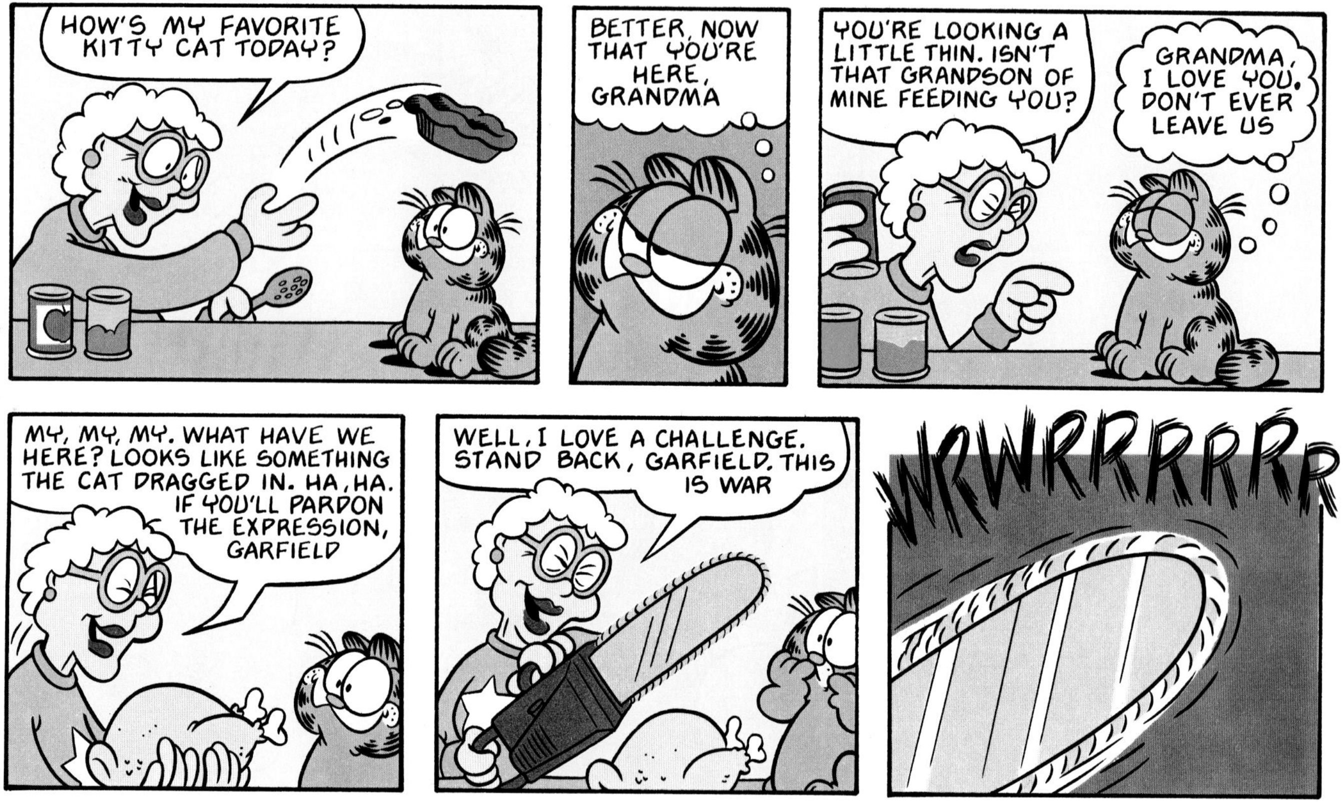
HOW'S MY FAVORITE KITTY CAT TODAY?
BETTER, NOW THAT YOU'RE HERE, GRANDMA
YOU'RE LOOKING A LITTLE THIN. ISN'T THAT GRANDSON OF MINE FEEDING YOU?
GRANDMA, I LOVE YOU. DON'T EVER LEAVE US
MY, MY, MY. WHAT HAVE WE HERE? LOOKS LIKE SOMETHING THE CAT DRAGGED IN. HA, HA. IF YOU'LL PARDON THE EXPRESSION, GARFIELD
WELL, I LOVE A CHALLENGE. STAND BACK, GARFIELD. THIS IS WAR
WRWRRRRRRR

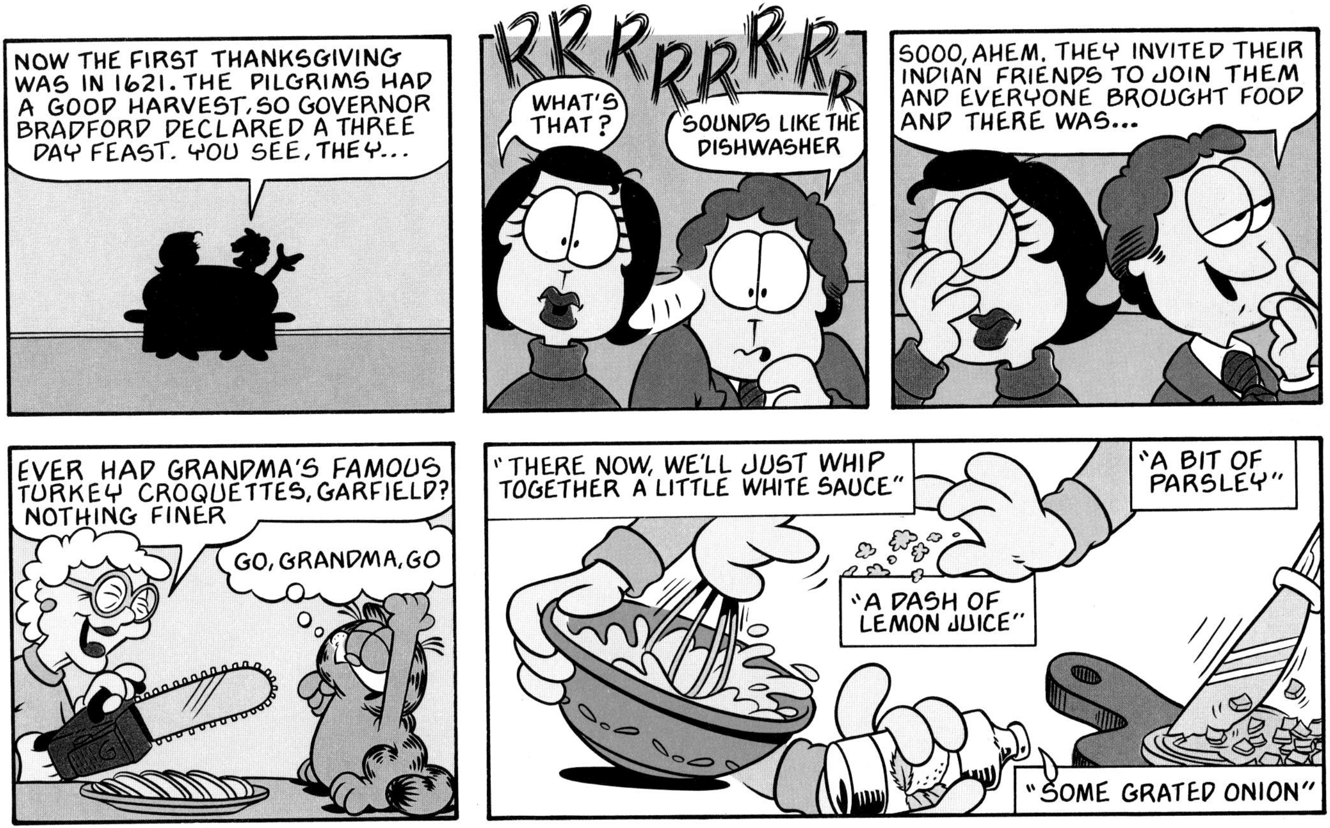

NOW THE FIRST THANKSGIVING WAS IN 1621. THE PILGRIMS HAD A GOOD HARVEST, SO GOVERNOR BRADFORD DECLARED A THREE DAY FEAST. YOU SEE, THEY...
RRRRRRRRR
WHAT'S THAT?
SOUNDS LIKE THE DISHWASHER
SOOO, AHEM. THEY INVITED THEIR INDIAN FRIENDS TO JOIN THEM AND EVERYONE BROUGHT FOOD AND THERE WAS...
EVER HAD GRANDMA'S FAMOUS TURKEY CROQUETTES, GARFIELD? NOTHING FINER
GO, GRANDMA, GO
"THERE NOW, WE'LL JUST WHIP TOGETHER A LITTLE WHITE SAUCE"
"A BIT OF PARSLEY"
"A DASH OF LEMON JUICE"
"SOME GRATED ONION"

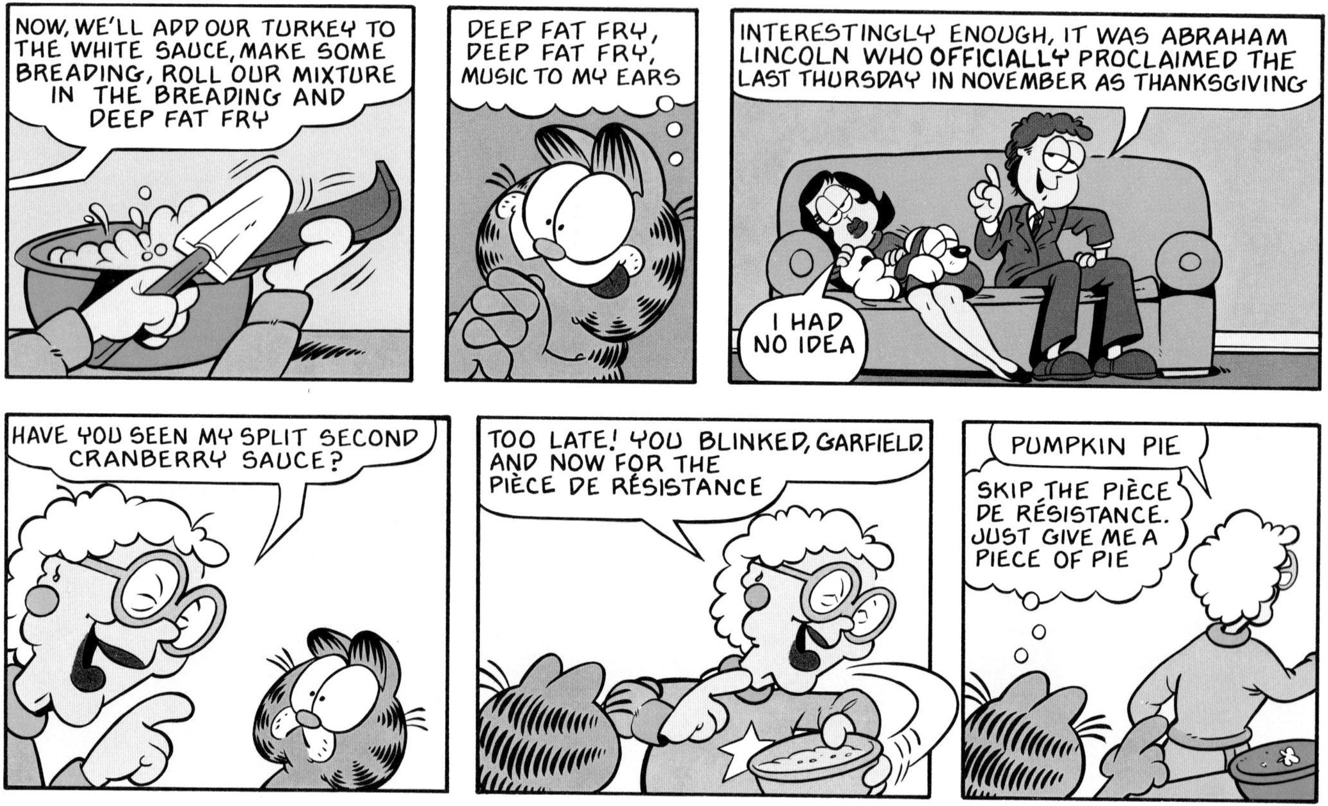
NOW, WE'LL ADD OUR TURKEY TO THE WHITE SAUCE, MAKE SOME BREADING, ROLL OUR MIXTURE IN THE BREADING AND DEEP FAT FRY
DEEP FAT FRY, DEEP FAT FRY, MUSIC TO MY EARS
INTERESTINGLY ENOUGH, IT WAS ABRAHAM LINCOLN WHO OFFICIALLY PROCLAIMED THE LAST THURSDAY IN NOVEMBER AS THANKSGIVING
I HAD NO IDEA
HAVE YOU SEEN MY SPLIT SECOND CRANBERRY SAUCE?
TOO LATE! YOU BLINKED, GARFIELD. AND NOW FOR THE PIÈCE DE RÉSISTANCE
PUMPKIN PIE
SKIP THE PIÈCE DE RÉSISTANCE. JUST GIVE ME A PIECE OF PIE

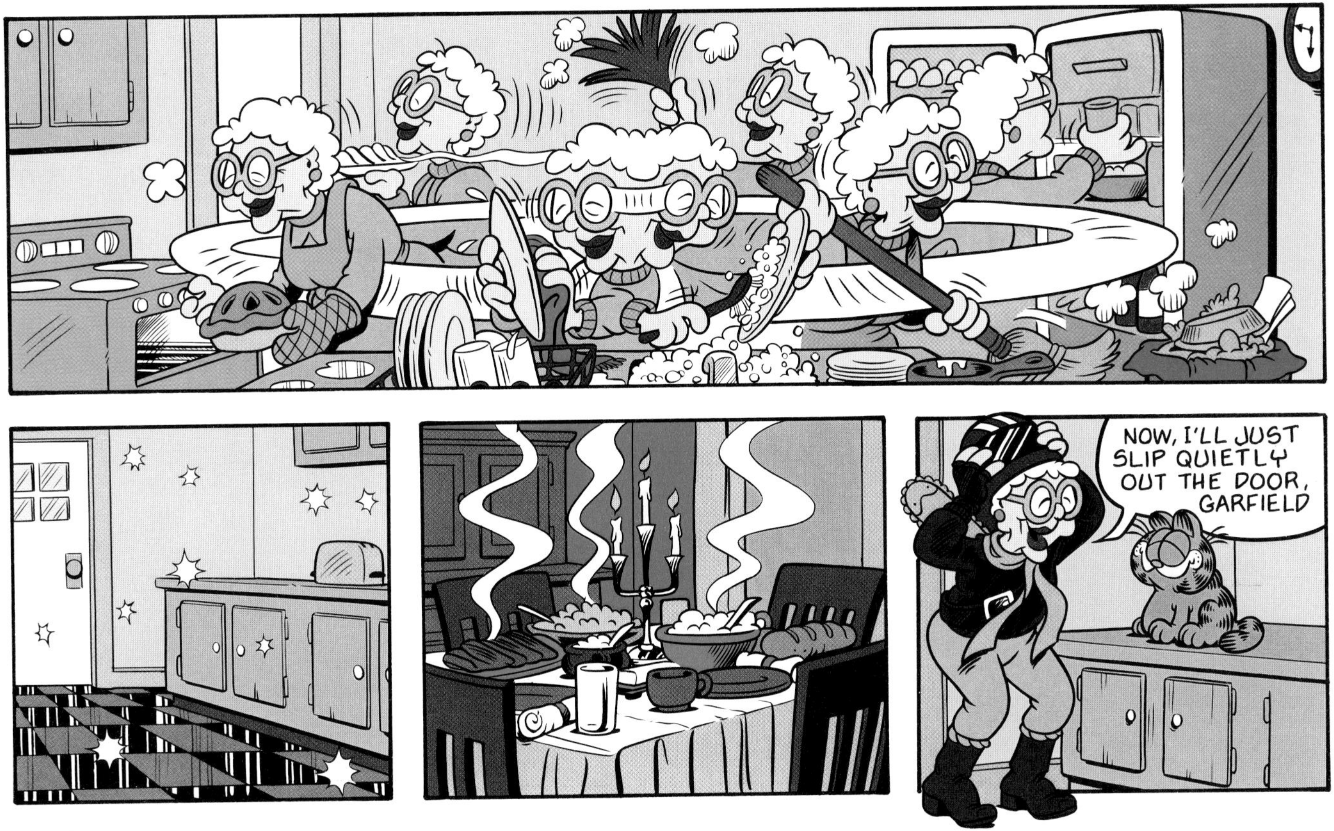
NOW, I'LL JUST SLIP QUIETLY OUT THE DOOR, GARFIELD

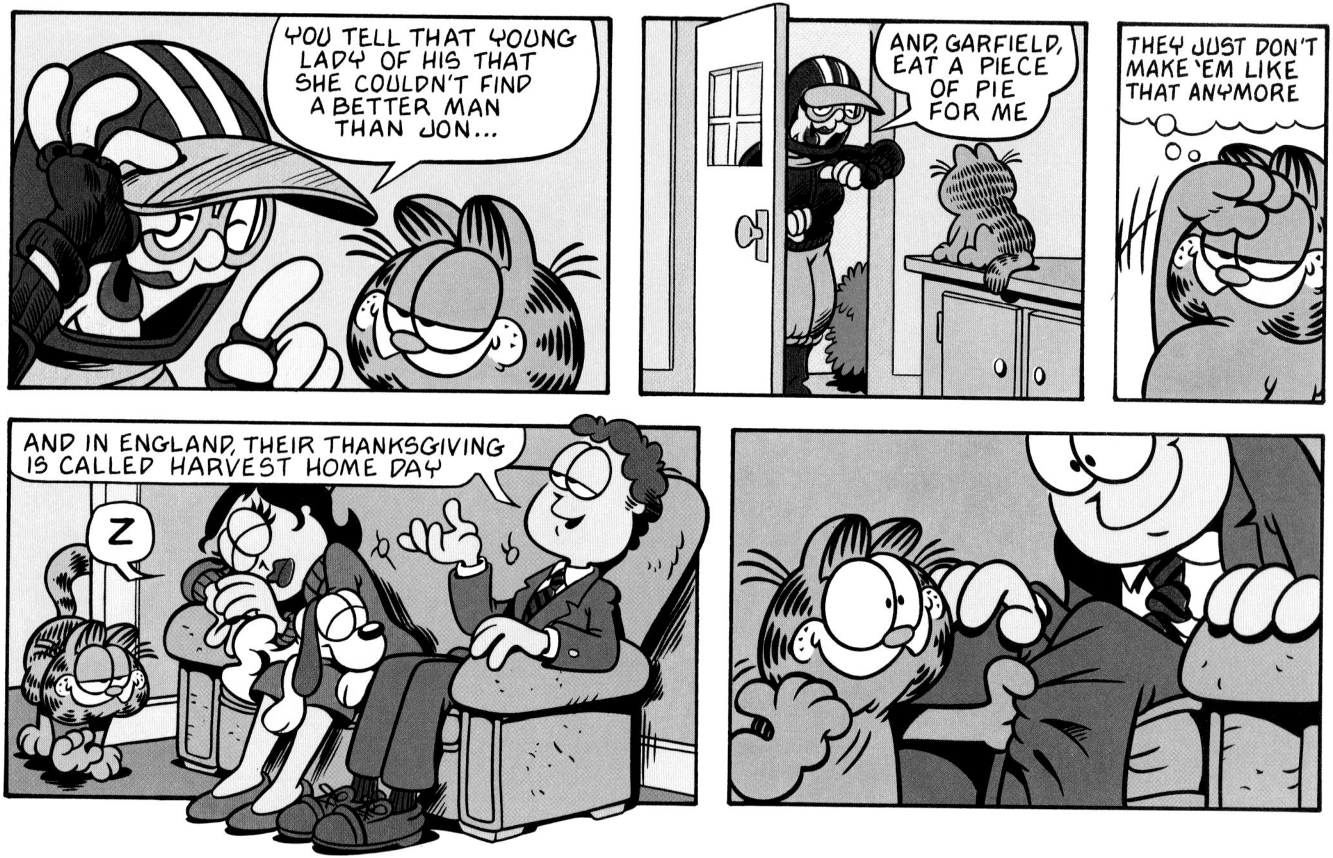
YOU TELL THAT YOUNG LADY OF HIS THAT SHE COULDN'T FIND A BETTER MAN THAN JON...
AND, GARFIELD, EAT A PIECE OF PIE FOR ME
THEY JUST DON'T MAKE 'EM LIKE THAT ANYMORE
AND IN ENGLAND, THEIR THANKSGIVING IS CALLED HARVEST HOME DAY
Z

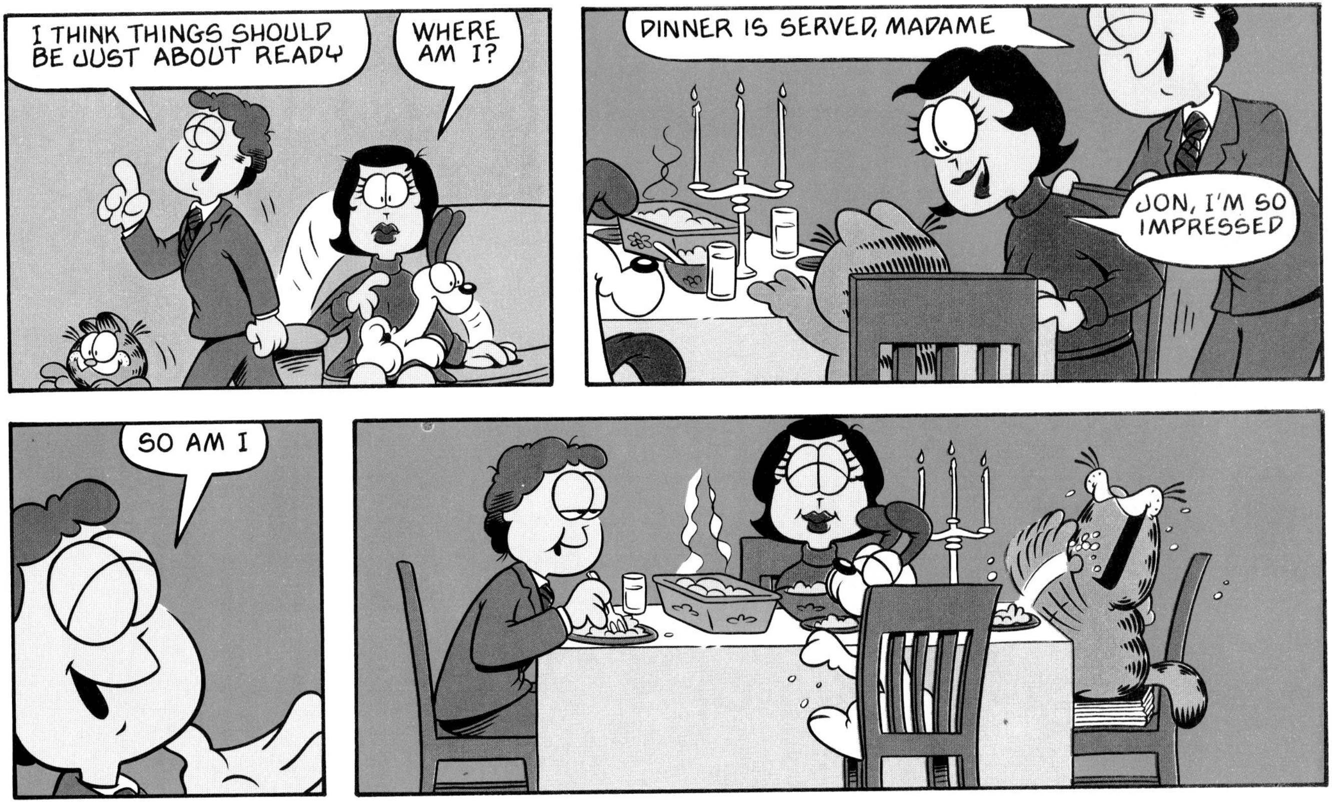
I THINK THINGS SHOULD BE JUST ABOUT READY
WHERE AM I?
DINNER IS SERVED, MADAME
JON, I'M SO IMPRESSED
SO AM I

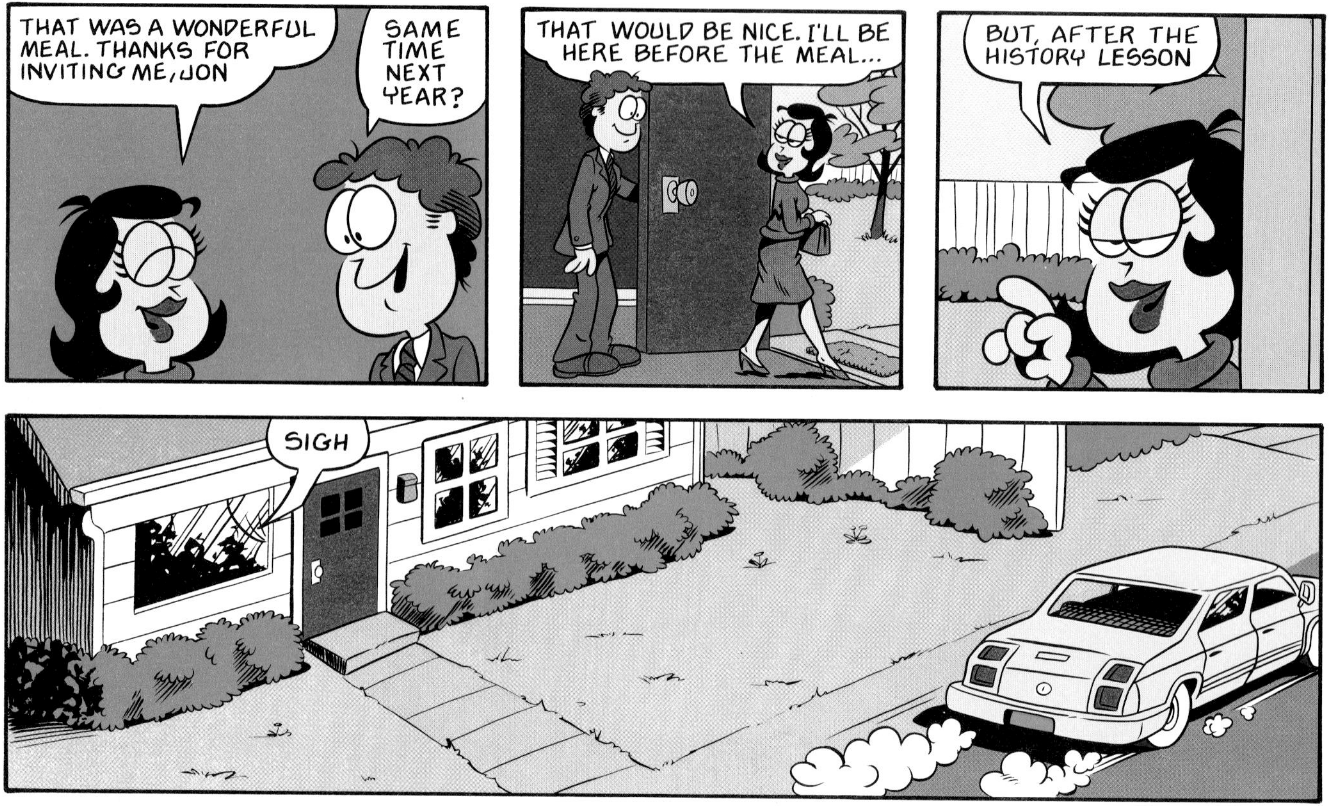
THAT WAS A WONDERFUL MEAL. THANKS FOR INVITING ME, JON
SAME TIME NEXT YEAR?
THAT WOULD BE NICE. I'LL BE HERE BEFORE THE MEAL...
BUT, AFTER THE HISTORY LESSON
SIGH

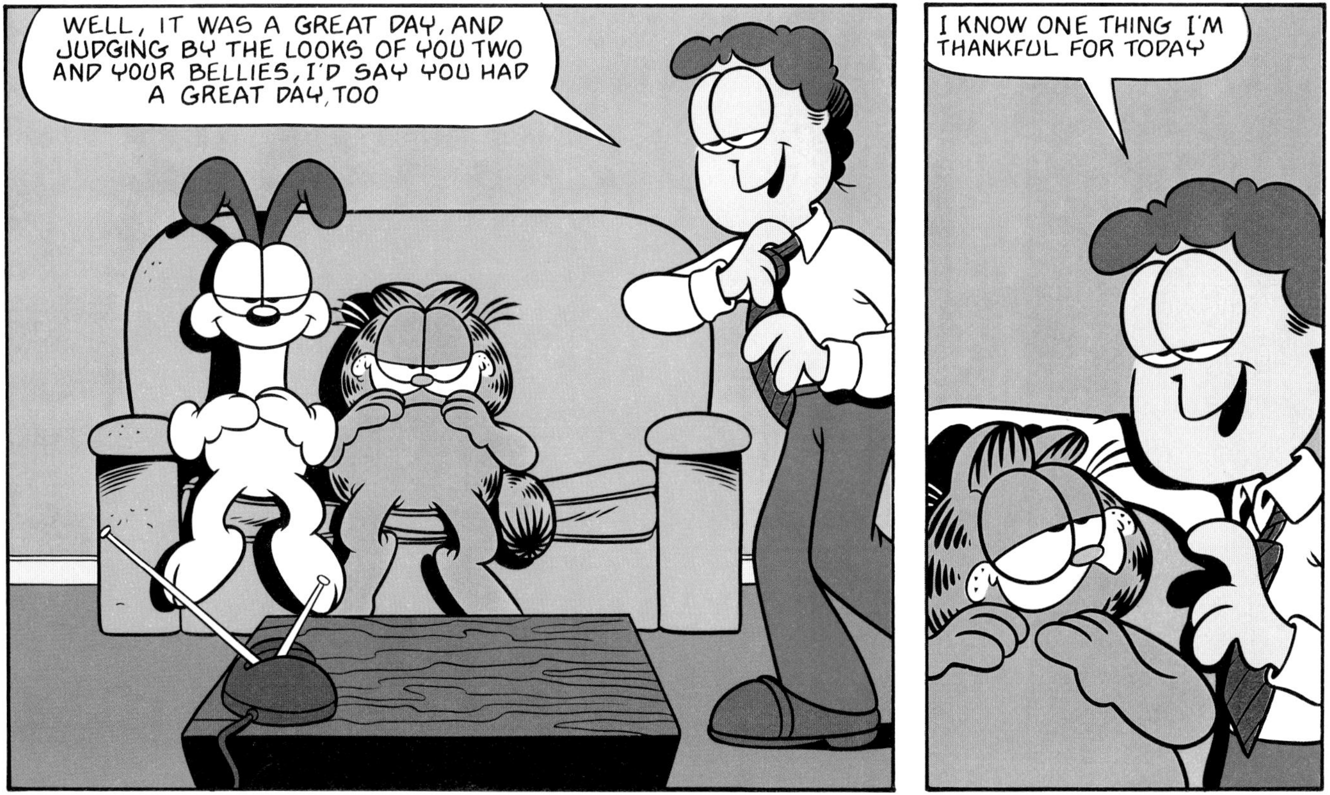
WELL, IT WAS A GREAT DAY, AND JUDGING BY THE LOOKS OF YOU TWO AND YOUR BELLIES, I'D SAY YOU HAD A GREAT DAY, TOO
I KNOW ONE THING I'M THANKFUL FOR TODAY

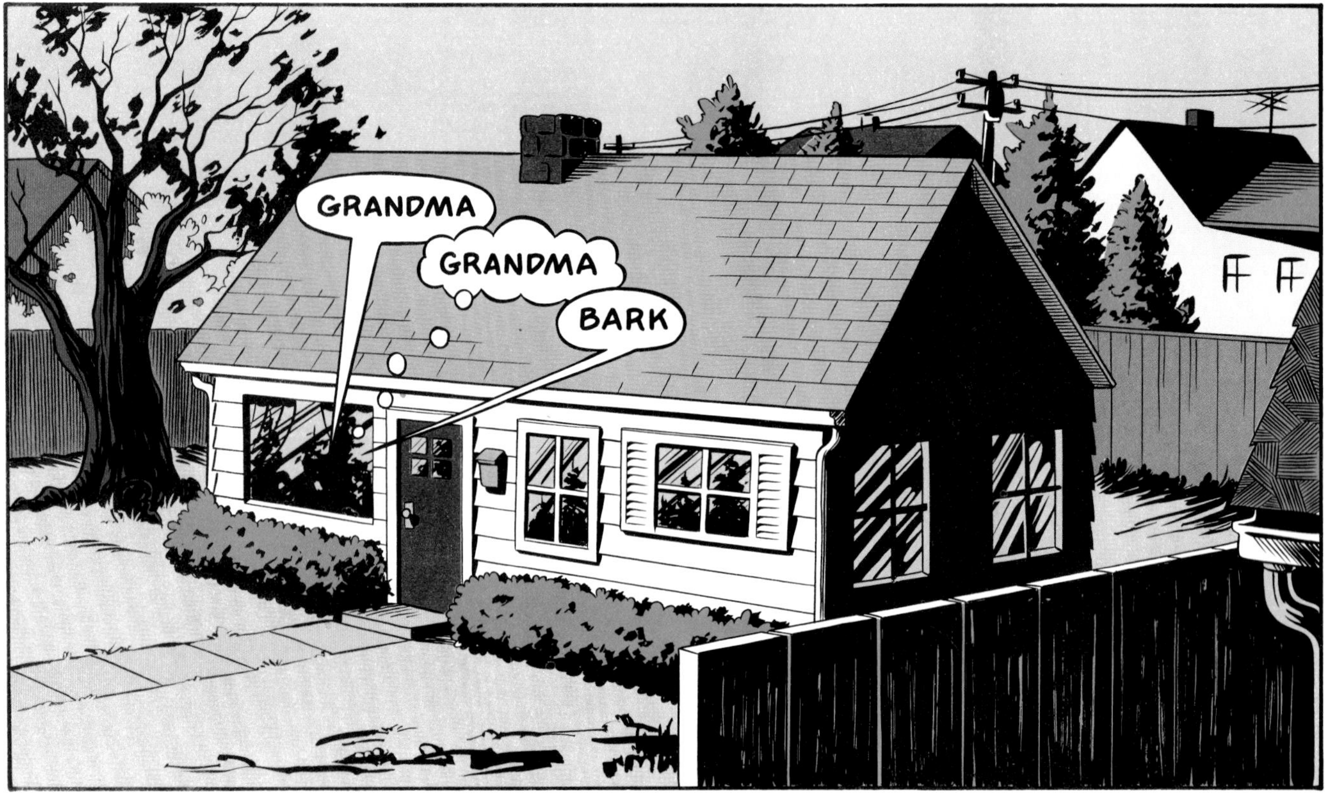
GRANDMA
GRANDMA
BARK